T2-CRY-106

THE
BETTER
WRITING
BREAKTHROUGH

THE BETTER WRITING

BREAKTHROUGH

Connecting Student Thinking and Discussion to Inspire Great Writing

FOREWORD BY **JOHN HATTIE**

ELEANOR DOUGHERTY
LAURA BILLINGS
TERRY ROBERTS

Alexandria, VA USA

1703 N. Beauregard St. • Alexandria, VA 22311-1714 USA
Phone: 800-933-2723 or 703-578-9600 • Fax: 703-575-5400
Website: www.ascd.org • E-mail: member@ascd.org
Author guidelines: www.ascd.org/write

Deborah S. Delisle, *Executive Director*; Robert D. Clouse, *Managing Director, Digital Content & Publications*; Stefani Roth, *Publisher*; Genny Ostertag, *Director, Content Acquisitions*; Carol Collins, *Senior Acquisitions Editor*; Julie Houtz, *Director, Book Editing & Production*; Liz Wegner, *Associate Editor*; Louise Bova, *Senior Graphic Designer*; Mike Kalyan, *Manager, Production Services*; Keith Demmons, *Production Designer*

Copyright © 2016 ASCD. All rights reserved. It is illegal to reproduce copies of this work in print or electronic format (including reproductions displayed on a secure intranet or stored in a retrieval system or other electronic storage device from which copies can be made or displayed) without the prior written permission of the publisher. By purchasing only authorized electronic or print editions and not participating in or encouraging piracy of copyrighted materials, you support the rights of authors and publishers. Readers who wish to reproduce or republish excerpts of this work in print or electronic format may do so for a small fee by contacting the Copyright Clearance Center (CCC), 222 Rosewood Dr., Danvers, MA 01923, USA (phone: 978-750-8400; fax: 978-646-8600; web: www.copyright.com). To inquire about site licensing options or any other reuse, contact ASCD Permissions at www.ascd.org/permissions, or permissions@ascd.org, or 703-575-5749. For a list of vendors authorized to license ASCD e-books to institutions, see www.ascd.org/epubs. Send translation inquiries to translations@ascd.org.

All referenced trademarks are the property of their respective owners.

All web links in this book are correct as of the publication date below but may have become inactive or otherwise modified since that time. If you notice a deactivated or changed link, please e-mail books@ascd.org with the words "Link Update" in the subject line. In your message, please specify the web link, the book title, and the page number on which the link appears.

PAPERBACK ISBN: 978-1-4166-1884-3   ASCD product #114010   n4/16
PDF E-BOOK ISBN: 978-1-4166-2147-8; see Books in Print for other formats.
Quantity discounts: 10–49, 10%; 50+, 15%; 1,000+, special discounts (e-mail programteam@ascd.org or call 800-933-2723, ext. 5773, or 703-575-5773). For desk copies, go to www.ascd.org/deskcopy.

Library of Congress Cataloging-in-Publication Data

Names: Dougherty, Eleanor, 1947- author.
Title: The better writing breakthrough: connecting student thinking and
    discussion to inspire great writing / Eleanor Dougherty, Laura Billings,
    Terry Roberts ; foreword by John Hattie.
Description: Alexandria, Virginia : ASCD, [2015] | Includes bibliographical
    references and index.
Identifiers: LCCN 2015043335 (print) | LCCN 2016000821 (ebook) | ISBN
    9781416618843 (pbk.) | ISBN 9781416621478 (PDF) | ISBN 9781416621461
    (Mobi) | ISBN 9781416621485 (Epub)
Subjects: LCSH: English language--Composition and exercises--Study and
    teaching.
Classification: LCC LB1576 .D638 2015 (print) | LCC LB1576 (ebook) | DDC
    372.6--dc23
LC record available at http://lccn.loc.gov/2015043335

25 24 23 22 21 20 19 18 17 16   1 2 3 4 5 6 7 8 9 10 11 12

THE BETTER WRITING BREAKTHROUGH

✦ ✦ ✦ ✦ ✦

Foreword
Lighting a Fire

When I graduated, one of my supervisors said, "Do not go out and be like most academics and study failure; instead, study success." Success is all around us, but so often we look for failure so we can then offer tidbits to make things better! Studying success requires the courage to say it is indeed success. Hence, when I was asked (cajoled, forced) by my dean to head an evaluation of the Paideia program that was being forcibly prescribed as the teaching method in all 90 schools in our district, I resisted because I did not want to study failure. The notion of compelling so many teachers to use a particular method was contrary to everything we know—teachers subvert forced innovations, act like magpies and take bits of a new teaching method into their own repertoire, and quickly revert to their own tried and known methods.

Reluctantly I went to Chapel Hill to meet these interlopers into our school district. The Paideia people, too, were nervous about a measurement person (me) being given some authority over their program. During the hour-long presentation, they claimed that the Paideia method would solve 166 of the district's problems—including absenteeism, social problems, and low engagement in learning—and, of course, increase test scores. Never had a program had such a hill to climb. I sat in anxious awe at what was demanded from one program developed by a small group of dedicated advocates!

The evaluation proceeded, and it was astonishing. I attended the compulsory workshops with many grumpy teachers who gave up their holidays to come back to school. Within moments, they were sitting up and engaging in the tasks, and soon a buzz was apparent. This method was new, straightforward, and adaptable to what they were already doing, and the results were so obviously positive. I recall later going into the class of one teacher whom I know to be among the worst teachers I have seen (she was my son's teacher), and even she had improved. The evidence was clear—there were major improvements to student involvement, test scores, and most of all, the depth of processing that students were using in their lessons.

Given what I witnessed, I thought I should try it myself. The Paideia method requires imparting knowledge and concepts about a third of the time. I finished my two-hour class on Messick's concept of validity feeling the warm glow of success. The activities were engaging, my wit was evident, students were enjoying the class, and they answered my questions. The next week I arranged them in a Socratic seminar, asked a stunning opening question, and then listened to students ask each other questions and provide answers. The hardest part was not intervening—I wanted to help them, and they wanted my guidance—but I was well trained to not step in. But then they asked the silliest questions and responded with the stupidest answers—what a sobering reflection on the lack of success of my teaching. I was a great teacher, but I was not so good at helping the students learn!

I then attended more Paideia classes by Terry Roberts and Laura Billings and became much better at combining the parts: I learned how to phrase good opening questions, how to shut up more, and how to use backward design to create better "coached products" to ensure my students worked on tasks more aligned with the various parts of the Paideia model. I stopped being a conductor of classes who coached answers out of students to reinforce my concept of myself as a teacher who could perform a marvelous monologue, and started listening to the impact of my role as a teacher.

Our conclusions about implementing Paideia in the district after the first year showed that Paideia had a firm foothold in the minds of principals, teachers, and students. We found important changes in classroom climate, more student engagement in dialogue and reductions in teacher monologues, student conceptions of learning that moved from learning to pass tests to learning to deepen understanding and enjoy learning, and greater confidence in the learning process. Students said that teachers who implemented Paideia were better at explaining information, ensured that students had a good understanding, expected more effort at working, were more likely to make students think, taught in interesting ways, and showed by example that learning is fun.

So why did it not continue? At the time, the state introduced a new test-based accountability model, and many of the most successful Paideia schools did not come out on top using this model. This is not surprising since the state tests were mainly favoring surface-level knowledge, and Paideia had a more appropriate mix of surface and deep thinking. The test model measured achievement, not progress, and thus favored those schools that entered with brighter students, whereas Paideia worked across all age groups and not just in the schools with the least or most advantaged students. The accountability method also found that the school leaders needed to be the best advocates to sustain the program and that teachers needed to work together within and across schools to evaluate their impact and improve their teaching (which was not funded).

I have watched the development of the Paideia method with high interest since these early experiences and indeed have just finished supervising an excellent PhD student who used social computer networking to implement Paideia. Davies (2015) found the Paideia method led to increased volume and complexity of student responses, especially on measures of student-to-student interaction.

So to be asked to write a foreword to their new book is a completion of the circle. Terry Roberts and Laura Billings taught me so much.

The focus of this book is related to writing—but the theme is thinking and talking about writing. They call this the Discourse and Writing Cycle, and it involves much more than saying, "Write an interesting story," which has turned off generations of students. In my more extreme moments, I would like to ban creative writing (at least in elementary school) and instead teach writing for a purpose—to persuade, instruct, narrate, describe, explain, or relate. This involves thinking about a text or topic *and* the audience of the writing. It involves discourse with others to check, clarify, evaluate, and confirm the writing. *The Better Writing Breakthrough* lights this spark: It asks teachers to conduct Paideia seminars so that "students are flush with both new thoughts and new language with which to express those thoughts." Then writing is the natural complement to formal classroom discourse, just as formal discourse is the natural prelude to writing.

While the book refers to the Common Core, the messages are more global and applicable to most curricula that value students expressing themselves in ways that allow others to see their thinking, appreciate their fluency in making compelling arguments, and enjoy seeing how others think and make meaning. The steps to teaching writing are well outlined and involve an unusual order—and this is worth reading this book. I particularly welcome the section on exemplar prompts since, as I discovered in my first trials with Paideia, developing open questions and exemplary prompts is not so straightforward. These sections are critical in this book.

In one of the most impressive meta-analyses ever completed, Murphy, Wilkinson, Soter, Hennessey, and Alexander (2009) asked about the role of classroom discussions in comprehension and learning. While their focus was reading, the messages can be translated to the teaching of writing. Murphy and colleagues were particularly interested in various approaches to conducting intellectually stimulating discussions that appear to be effective in promoting high-level responses to text. These approaches serve different but related purposes: The critical-analytic stance encourages a discussion in which the student's querying mind is engaged, prompting a more subjective, critical response toward the text. The knowledge acquisition approach focuses on reading and writing to acquire and promote particular information, with a focus on ideas, information, and conclusions. The aesthetic approach promotes affective responses.

Across their 42 studies, the average effect size was a huge .82, and this reinforces the emphasis in this book: the power of deliberate classroom discussion. For all three approaches there was an increase in student talk, a decrease in teacher talk, and an increase in students' literal and inferential comprehension, but overall there was much less effect on promoting students' critical thinking, reasoning, and argumentation about and around text. They noted that increases in student talk did not necessarily result in increases in student comprehension. The *focus* of the student talk (influenced by how the teacher set the discussion up) was more critical to promoting comprehension than reducing the amount of teacher talk.

They noted that classroom discussions were more potent for students of below-average ability, probably because students of higher ability levels already possessed the skills needed to comprehend narrative text. But this also suggests that these higher-ability students need a different type or focus of classroom talk.

Their conclusion was that not all discussion approaches are created equal. This is where *The Better Writing Breakthrough* takes off. It is not as simple as more student talk; it is a specifically guided and deliberate stance by the teacher in constructing dialogue, monitoring it (less intrusively than the usual tell-and-practice model), and learning from the teacher impact on the discussion to modify, augment, and sometimes stop and do different.

Most importantly, there is a time for the transition from the thinking to the writing phases. This is the essence of this book's contributions. The authors provide an impressively high level of advanced thinking and contributions for teachers, including advice on deconstructing the prompt and rubric, capturing the discourse, structuring a composition, and using outlining as thinking. They offer suggestions for developing the writing process, from crafting an opening section, to developing the statement of the ideas, to writing the first sentence and opening paragraph, to writing the first draft. Then they cover drafting, editing, publishing, and celebrating, including separate sections for different subject areas. Writing is communicating ideas, moods, and interpretations, and it does not need to be a unique process for each subject discipline. The audience may change, hence the purpose of writing may change, but the development of the writing process is similar.

Reading this book allows the mind to be on fire both as a reader and as a teacher, to the benefit of students. How often we dim or extinguish the sparks that can come from good writing! William Butler Yeats proclaimed that "Education is not the filling of a pail, but the lighting of a fire." This book lights the fire for the teaching of writing.

— John Hattie, author of the *Visible Learning* books

References

Davies, M. (2015). *Investigating the use of talk in classrooms to increase critical thinking, speaking, and writing* (Unpublished doctoral dissertation). University of Melbourne, Melbourne, Australia.

Murphy, P. K., Wilkinson, I. A. G., Soter, A. O., Hennessey, M. N., & Alexander, J. F. (2009). Examining the effects of classroom discussion on students' comprehension of text: A meta-analysis. *Journal of Educational Psychology, 101*(3), 740–764.

◆ ◆ ◆ ◆ ◆

Introduction
A Discourse Community

Without communication, there can be no community.

—Mortimer Adler, *How to Speak, How to Listen*

This is a book by teachers, for teachers—and those who lead them. Taken together, the three of us have 70-plus years of teaching experience, primarily in public middle and high school classrooms. Our teaching has taken place in five states in widely varied classroom settings, so our collective experience covers a lot of literal and figurative territory. The one thing we all have in common as a result of that experience, however, is a belief in and dedication to classroom discourse and writing as ways of thinking deeply about a subject. In fact, we know from experience and research that a discourse community engaged in speaking, listening, and writing is the one sure way to teach the concepts that are the foundation of any subject. The approach to teaching writing we present in this book is built on a specific form of discourse: the Paideia seminar, a prewriting experience to inspire you as a teacher of writing and to help you inspire your students to write with confidence and competence.

Two of us share a common experience with writing. We were taught to write in school by the old-fashioned method, and we suspect that many of you share that experience. In elementary school, we learned to read simple texts and suffered through rudimentary instruction in spelling, punctuation, and grammar. Grammar and punctuation practice grew in complexity as the grades passed by. Some of us stood in class and recited verb tenses by rote; some of us went to the board to diagram sentences. We learned not to split infinitives or begin a sentence with a conjunction. We even learned that subjects and verbs should agree—though about what we weren't certain.

Then one fateful day, a teacher slipped silently up behind us and yelled, "Write!" Somehow, each of us, struggling alone at a cold, hard school desk, was supposed to call all those words, punctuation marks, and grammatical constructions to order. We struggled to keep up with the waves of writing assignments to follow, and the red ink flowed freely from the teachers' pens onto our nascent efforts to compose.

What we also have in common is that while we had standard writing instruction, we had almost no instruction in how to participate in a focused, structured conversation. Although we all took part in what passed for traditional classroom discussion—in which the teacher drilled the class with closed questions and deemed which answers were correct—we never participated in what has come to be called Socratic or Paideia seminars. In other words, we were taught to write but not very well, and we weren't taught to speak and listen at all.

However, one of us did experience writing as discourse and learned that speaking with and listening to others before and during writing helped her develop an internal discourse throughout the writing process that she uses to this day.

As teachers, what we know now is also different from what we knew then. We know now that writing the way writers do is quite different from the grammar, punctuation, spelling, and yelling method. We also know that formal classroom discussion can teach students to think deeply about the curriculum. Finally, we are discovering that when we combine the two—formal discussion and the writing process—even reluctant writers can produce work of consistently high quality.

In particular, experience has taught us that the best way to empower less confident readers and writers is to give them something to think about, particularly the ideas and information presented in demanding texts. When students are faced with such texts (whether visual, print, or auditory), they have the opportunity to participate in active classroom discussions that motivate them and build their knowledge. As they hear a text discussed—and occasionally participate verbally—they are gleaning insights into the text as well as the language with which to express those ideas. If they then capture some of those ideas and some of that language on paper immediately following the seminar, they have the raw material with which to jump-start the writing process. Students who used to produce a few sketchy sentences in response to an essay prompt now have the capacity to put a lot more material on paper, material that can then be molded and reshaped into a much more complete piece of writing.

Although we reference the Common Core State Standards for English Language Arts, the principles and practices we advocate in this book apply to any curriculum that engages students in writing extended expository compositions grounded in texts of all types in grades 4–12. The underlying principles of instruction do not change throughout the grades, although the practices for teaching writing may vary in length and complexity as expectations for elaboration change. By the end of grade 4, students should be able to write multiple paragraphs in a focused and well-structured composition. By the end of 12th grade, students should have so internalized the practices, processes, and thinking that go into writing a composition that they are able to manage college assignments largely on their own.

Another important theme in this book is the role of discourse and writing in the core subjects. Whether you teach English, history or social studies, science, or math, writing instruction follows similar processes, although instruction should adjust for each discipline's contexts. When a school faculty teaches writing across the curriculum, teachers learn from each other as they share the hard work of crafting assignments, delivering instruction, and scoring student work. We have observed the same dynamic one coach described when he told us how he is learning that more ideas are emerging as teachers work together and how he enjoys working with students in other classes. In an e-mail to us, he said, "Kids rolled up their sleeves and worked on the writing assignment tied to a Florida Learning State Standard."

This book, then, is our gift to you—those who have struggled with us to teach struggling readers and reluctant writers of any age how to confront complex and demanding text. We have not provided you with a canned script, because we have too much respect for your own experience and insight. We have not written a workbook, because we trust you to study and apply the Discourse and Writing Cycle, reflect on the examples, and continue improving your own practice. You can neither learn these skills by rote nor teach them that way.

Instead, we have attempted to provide you with a trustworthy approach for teaching writing by involving students in a variety of texts and engaging in speaking and listening across all subjects—with a consistent focus on both discourse and writing as *thinking*. We do not elaborate on specific instructional methods, but we do focus on setting the stage for instruction that includes writing and discourse processes. The goal is to help you train your students to speak and write in language that is increasingly clear, coherent, and sophisticated—because their thinking is increasingly clear, coherent, and sophisticated. In this way, we hope that together we can produce a next generation of students (and teachers) for whom both conversation and writing are less painful and more rewarding.

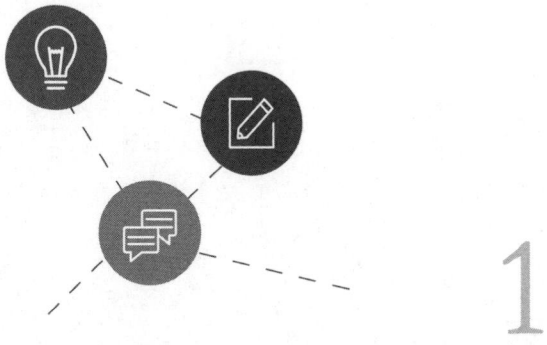

Discourse and Writing as Thinking

In Part 1 you will find two chapters to help you understand the power of teaching students to think critically by assigning them high-quality assignments involving reading, seminar discussion, and writing. We discuss the importance of pairing discourse with writing and provide a guide for designing writing assignments that require both rigorous literacy skills and content mastery.

1

Why Pair Discourse with Writing?

Nothing is to remain undiscussed. Everybody is to speak his mind. No proposition is to be left unexamined.

—Robert Maynard Hutchins, *The Great Conversation*

When classroom talk becomes an integral part of writing instruction, students benefit immeasurably. Their thinking and communication skills grow as part of a single process that connects speaking and listening with writing. The approach to teaching writing we describe in this book involves using a specific kind of discourse strategy, the Paideia seminar, in partnership with a traditional writing process. We call this method the Discourse and Writing Cycle (DWC). We also employ other discussion methods and "talk/write" activities to develop and support student thinking throughout the writing process.

Although our focus is primarily on writing, the DWC also provides opportunities to teach students reading comprehension and vocabulary building strategies as they prepare to discuss and write about a rigorous text. Our instructional approach derives from the understanding that reading is not only a skill but also an intellectual practice in which students engage in thinking about a text and using the full range of literacy practices: reading, writing, speaking and listening, and thinking. However, successfully conducting structured classroom discussions requires sufficiently investing in all students' speaking and listening skills. We use the term *discourse* to refer to a specific kind of structured talk that takes its cue from a text and the ideas and values in it. Sometimes this discourse takes the form of a discussion, conversation, or dialogue, and we may use these terms if the context fits. However, under the umbrella of discourse, students also use speaking and listening skills to exchange ideas. Discourse in a classroom occurs when a teacher provides a setting for interactions between and among peers that foster understanding.

To teach writing well also requires a significant investment of time because of the complexity of the writing process and the thinking it inspires. And yet, both 21st century skills inventories in general and the Common Core State Standards in particular are calling for a renewed commitment to teaching the full range of communication skills—including speaking and listening as well as writing—not just in English language arts classes but across the curriculum. In part, this book is a reply to that call. But more importantly, it is a handbook for teachers who honor all three communication skills as forms of critical thinking. The principles and practices we discuss in this book apply to writing instruction at any grade from upper elementary through high school, or roughly grades 4–12. The last section specifically addresses appropriate assignments for elementary, middle, and high school students.

READING, DISCUSSING, AND WRITING ABOUT COMPLEX TEXTS

One of the most important of the principles of DWC is the use of texts to provide the content for writing and to inspire the thinking that goes into writing. In this book, we make the "text" in all its various forms the focus of writing because texts engage students in the ideas and thinking central to the academic community and described in the Common Core English language arts standards. The high-quality texts that lend themselves to speaking, listening, and writing include print, visual, and auditory works that engage students in rich ideas or important information. We view speaking and listening skills as necessary for exploring thinking before, during, and even after students read and write. Structured discussions allow students to consider their and others' thoughts, make errors, and revise, in ways no other communication skills can. We forget that fluency in the spoken and written word is merely the outward sign of fluency in thought—and that we can't learn to think clearly without learning to speak, listen, and write well.

In an *Educational Leadership* article titled "Thinking Is Literacy, Literacy Thinking," we argued that

> *To teach thinking consistently . . . we should treat it as a funda-*
> *mental literacy skill, whether the language in question is algebra*
> *or English. There is no question that reading, writing, speaking,*
> *and listening are interconnected skills that develop synergisti-*
> *cally. They are also the key to teaching thinking. The more fluent*
> *students become as readers, writers, speakers, and listeners,*
> *the clearer, more coherent, and more flexible their thinking will*
> *become. (Roberts & Billings, 2008, p. 33)*

The profound connection between literacy and critical thinking helps clarify why both classroom discourse and writing should be consistently taught and practiced in school—and why that practice should take place in every subject area. This argument builds on the current focus on "disciplinary literacy" by asking teachers to teach a range of literacy skills—reading, speaking and listening, writing, and thinking—in addition to their subject area content. Advocates of disciplinary literacy are clear that if teachers want their students to think deeply about the curriculum—whether in math, science, history, or literature classes—then they must teach them to discuss the curriculum and write about it in ways consistent with each field of study. We are proposing that content area teachers teach speaking, listening, and writing skills (though not the mechanics of writing) in conjunction with subject area content, that is, that they help students become literate within their discipline.

The primary importance of discourse and writing in the classroom becomes clear if you accept that "learning to think . . . is the process of successfully explaining and manipulating increasingly complex texts" (Roberts & Billings, 2012, p. 1). As it is used here, *text* means any important artifact that is rich in ideas, whether a written text, map, painting, or photograph. The important thing is that students come to understand a text intellectually and be able to explain the concepts involved through speech and writing.

Another important lesson from a close study of literacy and thinking is the symbiotic relationship among the four primary literacy skills. Learning to write goes hand in hand with learning to read, speak, and listen. The core literacy skills are profoundly interdependent; indeed, it is all but impossible to write well without close reading and thoughtful discourse as part of the process. Of all the literacy skills, speaking well and writing well are the most closely related. For this reason, fluency in written language rarely occurs without a complementary fluency in spoken language.

Given the close connection between learning to express thoughts and learning to think, there are two main reasons why discourse and writing should be taught in all subject areas. The first is that by discussing and writing about the curriculum, students are thinking about the content with a depth and clarity that is difficult to achieve otherwise. The second is that learning to write—along with learning to read, speak, and listen—pays dividends throughout life. The first payoff comes in college, where students will be asked to write early and often, but that is only the beginning. Speaking, listening, and writing skills are also the key to success in most 21st century careers, because they are such an inherent part of critical thinking and because they are the means of communication with colleagues. For that reason, these skills are now more important than ever.

Although we emphasize writing that is expository and academic in nature, the assignment that follows a seminar can engage students in a variety of written products, ranging from traditional essays and reports to feature articles, memos, and interviews. No matter the product, however, there remain common expectations for clarity of thought and readability, so audience and purpose are always at the forefront of the writing task.

HOW DOES GROUP DISCOURSE INFLUENCE INDIVIDUAL WRITING?

As you will see more clearly in Chapter 3, we believe that classroom discourse needs to be a formal and deliberate process, like that of any other extended teaching strategy that is practiced over time. Students engage in discourse in a variety of forms, including seminars, conferences, small-group work, or whole-class conversations that are purposeful and intellectual. We base our classroom work in this book on the Paideia seminar, defined as "a collaborative, intellectual dialogue facilitated with open-ended questions about a text" (Roberts & Billings, 2003, p. 16). One of the key goals of this kind of discourse is that every student learns to participate in a reflective, self-aware manner. As a result, students of all ages consistently grow in both their speaking and listening skills and their intellectual understanding of the curriculum.

As we wrote in a book titled *Teaching Critical Thinking: Using Seminars for 21st Century Literacy*:

> *The depth and quality of the understanding reflected in a given seminar discussion is directly related to the depth and quality of the understanding that grows up in the minds of the individuals present. The individual mind is inspired by the group, and the group is inspired by the individual mind. If those involved are skilled enough . . . the result is a synthesis of multiple perspectives that is more sophisticated and explains more of the world than any one person's insight did in the beginning. (Roberts & Billings, 2012, p. 51)*

After a rich seminar discussion, students are flush with both new thoughts and new language with which to express those thoughts. Hearing students share their thoughts during a seminar often causes teachers to see those students in a new light.

Group discourse feeds individual thinking most powerfully when it is followed by individual writing, so that all students have a chance to develop what they heard, said, and thought during the seminar. This development is most effective when it is extended through the writing process, so that students have the opportunity to continue thinking about a complex text as they design, draft, revise, and even edit their writing. Their own thinking becomes increasing clear and, at the same time, increasingly sophisticated. Seen in this light, writing is the natural complement to formal classroom discourse just as formal discourse is the natural prelude to writing. This fundamental relationship is the focus of this book and the rationale for the Discourse and Writing Cycle (see Figure 1.1) that we explore here.

Figure 1.1		
The Discourse and Writing Cycle		
Discourse Sequence	**Transition to Writing Sequence**	**Writing Sequence**
a. Pre-Seminar Process b. Seminar Discussion c. Post-Seminar Process	d. Capturing the Discussion e. Structuring the Writing	f. Crafting an Opening g. Writing an Initial Draft h. Revising a Draft i. Editing and Publishing

HOW CAN WE CREATE A DISCOURSE AND A WRITING CULTURE IN ALL CLASSROOMS?

A culture of true discourse and extended writing is an intellectual culture—one of both exploration and reflection, characterized by the ongoing formative assessment of students' speaking, listening, and writing skills as well as the thinking that drives those skills. To say that a discourse and writing culture is intellectual means that it addresses the ideas and values that undergird the curriculum. In this way, the partnership between discourse and writing simultaneously challenges students to think more deeply about a topic and to find the language to express those thoughts.

To say that the process is characterized by ongoing formative assessment means that teachers and students are together engaged in using the process to improve each student's discussion and writing skills through every stage in the process and from unit to unit through the course. The result is speech and writing that is increasingly clear, coherent, and sophisticated.

According to researchers, writing assignments in the K–12 schools tend to be personal essays, imaginative writing, and journal writing—too few of the expository essays students will be asked to produce in college or the workplace (Applebee & Langer, 2013). These anecdotal and research data suggest that public schools are requiring less and less in-depth discussion and writing and that the writing they do assign tends to be more personal narrative than academic argument. Part of the reason for this devolution can be traced to the limitations imposed by standardized testing: a reliance on short essays and timed essays as benchmarks of assessment.

What, then, is required for the paradigm shift that would result in classrooms that truly prepare students for the demands of college and career?

1. First, teachers need to give up the mistaken notion of either discourse or writing as merely a method of evaluation, for that leads to teacher-dominated discussion plus short answers and timed essays as the only writing in most classrooms. Rather, teachers need to **treat both discourse and writing as process,** for that enhances students' literacy skills and leads to a more profound understanding of the curriculum. The goal should be that students learn the curriculum through discussing and writing about it, with each stage in the process leading to more sophisticated understanding.

2. Second, teachers need to begin to **emphasize expository writing,** because that is both the kind of writing that helps students understand the curriculum and what will be required of them in high school and beyond. Although narrative writing does have its place, and all good writing has some narrative qualities, teachers need to return to teaching expository writing as a strategy for teaching the curriculum. In particular, students need to do more expository writing as they move through the middle school years. By high school

they should be producing strong argumentative essays on a regular basis.

3. Third, teachers need to **embrace writing combined with classroom discourse** as the most dependable means of teaching the conceptual curriculum. If teachers want to teach students to think, then it is mandatory that teachers facilitate the Discourse and Writing Cycle in all subject areas. The assumption that discussion or writing is solely the responsibility of the language arts teacher is obsolete. In short, teachers desperately need to teach discourse along with writing in all subject areas.

FOR WHAT DOES DISCOURSE AND WRITING PREPARE US?

If you are in a Common Core state, the standards are clear on at least two of the three shifts in classroom instruction that we list above. The introductory material to the English language arts standards quotes the "Distribution of Communicative Purposes by Grade in the 2011 NAEP Writing Framework" to emphasize that literacy is the business of every teacher in the building and that "instruction in reading, writing, speaking, listening, and language [is] a shared responsibility within the school" (National Governors Association Center for Best Practices & Council of Chief State School Officers, 2010a, p. 4). These two elements in the Common Core reflect the growing conviction in the business community and elsewhere that communication and thinking skills are necessary for success in the 21st century workplace. Literacy skills are, in a sense, the *new* basics—in terms of both college and career.

They are also the *old* basics. We could venture far back in time to quote philosophers who link language with thought and prescribe fluency in both as preparation for life. More recently, in a series of books written in the 1980s, philosopher Mortimer Adler and the Paideia Group wrote "that the three callings for which schooling should prepare all [students] are, (a) to earn a decent livelihood, (b) to be a good citizen of the nation and the world, and (c) to make a good life for one's self" (1988, p. 310). Learning to discuss and to write—and therefore, to think—is an essential ingredient in the kind of schooling Adler is talking about. Not only is learning to communicate the proper preparation for college and career; it is also preparation for something even more important. It is preparation for a good life.

USING DISCOURSE IN THE WRITING PROCESS

To capitalize on the relationship between discourse and writing, we describe a cycle that imbues the traditional writing process with discourse methods, specifically the Socratic seminar, to help students develop their thinking about a topic and use their literacy skills to communicate their thinking. This pairing of discourse and writing is designed to combine the most productive aspects of classroom discussion with the traditional writing process.

By 4th grade, students should have acquired skills in structuring a basic composition in response to reading texts on a topic of three or more paragraphs and know that they have different purposes when writing argumentative and explanatory compositions. As they move up the grades, they develop their skills in fluency and elaboration that allow them to become more precise in their use of language, more logical, and more able to adapt their writing to a variety of audiences. But the basic 4th grade essay structure remains the same: opening, development, closing. Discourse throughout their years as student writers helps them develop the language and thought processes that result in clear, purposeful written products.

The DWC assignment plan is where teachers set the stage for the pairing of discourse and writing. This pairing aims to engage—and inspire—students more fully while simultaneously teaching them to think about what they have read as a means to write more powerfully. Figure 1.2 maps the dynamic between the DWC writing stages in an instructional plan that crosses over to critical-thinking skills. That is, the chart reminds you that you are teaching writing *as* critical thinking and using discourse to develop those connections. You may want to refer to this chart in the following chapters to reinforce this dynamic. Now, let's turn to Chapter 2 to plan and craft an effective DWC writing assignment.

Figure 1.2		
DWC Thinking Demands and Writing Skills		
Thinking Skills	**DWC Stages**	**Writing Skills**
Distinguish textual evidence that is appropriate for the assignment.	Capturing the Discussion	Read explicitly; skim and scan; use annotation and note-taking methods.
Determine and sequence a line of thought or logic to develop explanation or argument.	Structuring the Writing	Outline a structure using a method that sequences points or reasons.
Determine a credible claim or thesis; frame a relevant context for composition.	Crafting an Opening	Write a credible claim or thesis; provide relevant context.
Link points or ideas; connect relevant examples or citations to controlling idea.	Writing an Initial Draft	Construct a multiparagraph composition with an opening, development, and closing; use quotes, citations.
Check for logic, explanations, or reasoning; ensure statements are accurate; articulate a coherent line of thought.	Revising a Draft	Apply techniques to improve sentence fluency, language usage, logic, and use of supporting material.
Employ grammar and conventions to create meanings.	Editing and Publishing	Use correct spelling, punctuation; use correct citation formats; apply discipline-based protocols; present composition in a readable format.

2

Crafting an Effective DWC Assignment

Writing represents a unique mode of learning—not merely valuable, not merely special, but unique.

—Janet Emig, "Writing as a Mode of Learning," in *College Composition and Communication*

As Emig suggests, writing is different from speaking. It requires a more ordered and permanent articulation than speaking. However, speaking enables writing by presenting opportunities to explore expression and thought before putting pen to paper, and listening enables students to hear how others use language and develop thought. The key to teaching writing is to teach students strategies for transforming their talk into writing, and in the process teach thinking, because writing forces thinking in a way speaking does not. This dynamic among speaking, listening, and writing begins with an assignment. In this chapter, you will learn the principles and practices that will allow you to create a high-quality assignment: that is, one that engages students in writing in response to texts and uses discourse to develop their thinking. The Discourse and Writing Cycle, as described in Chapter 1, involves three sequences of instruction: the Discourse,

Transition to Writing, and Writing Sequences. The DWC assignment sets the stage for these three sequences because it shapes the charge to students.

You might wonder why we don't ask you to plan the Discourse Sequence first since you will eventually teach it first, and the answer is that you need the assignment prompt to determine the content of the seminar, which includes the text and the questions for the discussion. The assumption we make is that you teach students to read a text (this applies mostly to written texts) for a basic understanding before you begin teaching the DWC assignment. They should have some grasp of the topic and some idea of the line of thought. Use whatever methods work for you and your students so that they at least have a general understanding of the text; they will gain a deeper understanding during the seminar. The seminar precedes actual writing but prepares students for the reasoning and expression they will bring to their writing. However, it is not the only classroom discourse that takes place; after drafting a piece, students need further discussion to explore, modify, and revise the ideas and language in the writing. Talking leads to writing, which leads to talking, and so on.

This notion that talking helps students write emerged as a theory when Robert Zoellner (1969) and Terry Radcliffe (1972) proposed that student writing is enhanced when students engage in discussion as part of the process. In these and other studies, talking while writing involved peer-to-peer talk as well as teacher and student conferencing. From these studies, practitioners have developed discussion methods, such as "accountable talk," to help students work through their ideas (Burke, 2003; Fisher, Frey, & Rothenberg, 2008). Your goal is to become adept at writing high-quality assignments, including the prompt and the instructional plan, because they support students' efforts to perform at their best. You will be able to judge the success of your writing assignment because students will reflect your expectations successfully in their work.

However, in order to create a context for writing, you need to present students with an assignment prompt that tells them what to write about—a topic, a question, an issue, or an argument. The first step in planning a full literacy cycle consisting of both seminar and writing sequences is to craft an assignment that both motivates and inspires students to write and involves them in a specific context—an example of beginning with the end in mind. Keep in mind that an assignment is a component of a unit in which students focus on specific content and skills; it is not a unit in itself. Use an assignment to create a context in which students think about your content in a specific way and apply literacy skills to demonstrate their understanding. You will use the text and key questions about the text in the prompt as the basis for your seminar, so it's important to craft the assignment prompt before you plan the seminar in Chapter 3.

WHAT IS AN ASSIGNMENT?

One high school teacher noted, "I see now that we have to look at what we are teaching and come up with the assignment so we understand our overall endgame. And then we create the lesson plans to help us get to where we want to go. It seems so simple when I say it, but that is not what we are doing."

A successful academic writing assignment centers around an idea embedded in disciplinary content. A fully designed assignment contains four elements:

- A **prompt** based on standards or other learning goals
- A **product** as evidence of learning (e.g., ask students to analyze a science article's evidence, make a scale model, write an essay about a theme, or present an exhibit to a community organization)
- A **rubric,** which clarifies a prompt by stating detailed expectations
- An **instructional plan,** which notes the steps teachers take to deliver the Discourse, Transition to Writing, and Writing Sequences in the cycle

Note that the key difference between an assignment and a quiz, exam, or homework is that an assignment sets the stage for teaching, not testing. An assignment is taught step by step to enable students to acquire and refine the skills necessary to communicate their thinking in writing. When we start to work with teachers, we often find that they have only a vague idea of what an assignment is. With practice they understand, as one teacher put it, that an assignment has "instructional architecture."

The instructional architecture of a DWC assignment aims to create an environment for teaching students how to read closely and then to communicate in writing what they have read. The prompt sets the charge, and the instructional plan is designed to lead students through the writing sequence to produce a high-quality product in response to one or more texts. The connection between close reading and high-quality writing is well documented as "similar processes of meaning construction" (Olson, 2003, p. 17). An assignment successfully connects reading to writing when it provides students with guidance through the meaning-making process that leads to a written product. Most writing assignments in school are academic in that they require students to demonstrate discipline-specific protocols and strategies in their compositions. For example, a lab report requires specific structure and components, as does a proposal or an essay. Essay and journalistic writing requires certain formats, tone, and language ranging from more formal to less formal. Over a school year, writing assignments in the core and elective courses should expose students to a variety of assignments in order to help them learn to make the adjustments in their writing necessary to fit a variety of audiences and purposes. When you craft a series of assignments, you also control the trajectory of learning in your classroom as your assignments ask for increasingly sophisticated responses.

According to Lindsay Matsumura, crafting a "high-quality assignment involves many aspects of instruction and of student learning—from choosing texts to providing written comments on drafts of students' work" (2005, p. 1). The first of those aspects is the prompt with which an assignment begins, a statement that focuses on a topic or question and requires students to respond in some way. A quality prompt

- Engages students in writing in response to reading or research.
- Has a clear purpose aligned to curriculum standards.

- Is concise and consists of a few sentences.
- Is doable within a reasonable amount of time.

In contrast, a prompt that lacks relevant purpose and is unclear creates confusion for students and discourages their efforts to write. You can tell whether a prompt communicated what you intended by analyzing a class set of student work. If students are not responding in the way you had wanted, then it may be that your prompt isn't clear enough or students found it irrelevant.

To write a prompt, you can start with any one of the first four elements: content, learning goals, product, or text. In our sample, we start with content; however, all four elements in the steps should be in place in the final prompt statement.

Step 1: Identify Content Worth Teaching

One way to think about content worth teaching is to decide which of the several topics in a unit is worth spending one or more weeks writing about. Writing is an intensive experience for both teachers and students and requires time to think and produce, so identify content—especially key ideas and values—that allows you to teach not only topic-specific content but also universal or transferable concepts. For example, an assignment that focuses on the impact of tone by listening to and reading a speech by the late Texas Representative Barbara Jordan teaches students a lot about the importance of tone in general, especially when the audience is public and the topics are political. They can apply this knowledge to other speeches and texts. Refer to your content standards or scope and sequence for ideas. At this point you are thinking in broad terms. For example,

- In English, the theme of heroics in literature
- In history, the "isms" that influenced an era or event
- In science, a question about the impact of some science event or condition, such as pollution on plant life
- In arts, the use of an artistic style or method, such as perspective in early paintings

- In tech class, why and how something works, as in the functions of the components of a computer

Step 2: Identify a Learning Goal

A learning goal consists of a small cluster of standards or objectives that inform not only *what* you want students to address but *how*. Since we are focused on formal discussion and writing in response to reading, we form a cluster from a reading standard, a speaking and listening standard, and a writing standard, in addition to a content standard, when we build a prompt. You may address aspects of other standards during your instruction, but a cluster constitutes the focus that determines the assignment's topic and demands.

An example of a cluster taken from the Common Core English language arts standards is R.9, W.2, and SL.1. A prompt written to address this cluster would involve students in writing an explanatory essay in which they explain how "two or more texts address similar themes or topics in order to build knowledge or to compare the approaches the authors take" (National Governors Association Center for Best Practices & Council of Chief State School Officers, 2010a, p. 35). To demonstrate skills in speaking and listening, they might provide an oral summary for the class or participate in a seminar as a transition from reading to writing.

Step 3: Identify One or More Texts

The text you choose is all-important because it not only serves as the text for a seminar but must also allow students to apply the thinking and skills you have chosen when you identified content, mode, and learning goals. A text can be a print, visual, or auditory text, and it makes learning more interesting if students occasionally write about a painting, film clip, or data chart. We suggest that one or two short, profound texts will allow you to teach content and skills at a deep level and make the assignment manageable for you and your students. Examples of short, profound written texts are Lincoln's Second Inaugural Address, Sojourner Truth's "Ain't I a Woman?," and the anonymous but often sung Spanish love poem "Sólo Tú." You can select a chapter in a novel or a passage from long works. You will know a text is profound because it requires multiple readings and in-depth discussion. (See Chapter 3 for more discussion about selecting texts.)

Of course, students should also write research papers, but be aware that research requires a different set of reading and writing skills. Reading when researching a topic involves synthesizing multiple sources of information, requiring skills in reading quickly through texts to identify the usefulness of a text and then to read for information specific to a charge. In contrast, reading a single text closely to analyze a specific element requires students to slow down and reread in order to extrapolate meaning and to identify the author's use of an element. Whatever strategies students apply should enable them to discuss their thinking about the texts in writing. When you also teach with discourse, you help students digest and consider what they have read. Clearly, texts that are complex in theme help students stretch their thinking in any discipline and make writing a composition more interesting (Billings & Roberts, 2012–2013).

Step 4: Determine the Rhetorical Mode

The mode is the rhetorical purpose: most commonly to explain, inform, argue, or narrate. Each mode requires a unique set of writing demands. Most academic writing in secondary grades is analytical, whether students defend a claim or explain a concept or narrate historical event. Argumentation requires students to make a claim and convince the reader in their response, so a strong argument depends on sound reasoning. Language in your prompt such as "which," "is," "does," "argue," and "take a position" signals to students that they are writing in the argumentation mode. Editorials and critiques are examples of products that require students to argue for or against something. They must decide on a claim and provide relevant evidence for their positions. Prompts that require students to explain use language such as "how," "what," "analyze," and "compare." Reports and summaries are examples of explanatory products. Nonfiction narration (e.g., memoirs, biographies) requires students to relate something or give an account of an event, for example, and employ narrative strategies. Language such as "when," "tell," "relate," and "show" can signal that students write a chronology or provide the facts related to an event. The text should also allow you to teach the literacy standards you identified in Step 2.

Step 5: Identify the Product

The product is the student's written composition, of which there are several types. Each type or product signals to students an audience, whether academic or public, and an appropriate language register, from formal to informal. Some products also work exclusively with the mode you choose, so that's why we discuss mode before product.

For example, an editorial is almost always an argumentative or opinion product, while an essay might be either explanatory or argumentative. Essays are the most common form of academic composition, so your students should learn that the term *essay* signals a formal academic composition consisting of multiple paragraphs in which students state a controlling idea, support it with evidence from texts or sources, and provide a closing. A report is most often used in science, business, and journalism or for explanatory types of writing; like the essay, it is a multiparagraph composition. An editorial signals a wider audience, as for a newspaper, and is usually argumentative. A script requires students to apply conventions of written dialogue and pacing. The point here is that when you designate a product, you determine the skills you will need to teach. A science teacher who thought it would be fun to have students write a script about a health issue changed her mind when we pointed out that she would have to teach script format and conventions. She decided instead to craft an assignment in which students researched the topic and wrote a report, but she collaborated with the drama teacher to create a follow-up writing assignment that involved a script on the topic.

Step 6: Write a Prompt That Incorporates Steps 1–5

Now that you have determined the main elements of your prompt, it's time to put all these thoughts together in a written statement. Not all prompts involve a direct question, but it's implied or stated in most cases. However, a fully developed prompt further clarifies the product and demands. The questions in the examples below are derived from national organizations. We have elaborated on the questions to provide you with fully developed examples of a prompt.

What is the theme of "Mother to Son"? After reading "Mother to Son," write an essay for our class literary magazine in which you discuss how Langston Hughes's use of metaphors contributes to an understanding of the theme of this poem. Give several examples from the poem to support your discussion. (Elementary School [Feldman & Pittock, n.d.])

How does the writer effectively convey the context and feelings of the narrative voice? After reading and discussing Chapter 1 in Annie Dillard's Pilgrim at Tinker Creek, write an analysis in which you address the question and provide evidence from the text. (High School)

What do we mean by length, area, capacity, and volume? Read and discuss the article "What DO We Mean by Length, Area, Capacity, and Volume?" Write a brief explanation in which you define the terms and explain whether length, area, capacity, and volume are "fixed" metrics. Support your discussion with evidence from the text. (Middle School)

What does this story suggest about the power of individual will as compared to the effect of laws? After reading and discussing James Baldwin's Blues for Mister Charlie, write an essay in which you examine how individual will and power interact in the play. Support your discussion with evidence from the text. (Middle School)

What factors fostered the emergence of "republican motherhood" and the "cult of domesticity"? After reading and discussing the following texts, write an essay in which you explain each term and relate it to the political environment of the times. Support your discussion with evidence from the texts. (High School)

One resource to help you develop prompts is the Literacy Design Collaborative's collection of templates aligned with the Common Core. (For a full list of prompt templates, visit www.ldc.org and click on Resources.) For example:

Task 1E1: *[Insert optional question] After reading _____ (literature or informational texts), write _____ (an essay, report, or substitute) in which you define_____ (term or concept) and explain _____ (content). Support your discussion with evidence from the text(s).* **(Informational or Explanatory/Definition)**

The National Paideia Center website (www.paideia.org) also provides assignment prompts and lesson plans that include seminars.

We would like to pause here to reconsider what makes an effective prompt because the prompt is so important for creating the context for the next steps: writing a rubric and instructional plan.

What makes an effective DWC assignment prompt? In brief, an effective DWC prompt is a clearly written statement focusing on a topic or question about one or more texts. The DWC prompt should involve the same text discussed in the seminar and the ideas and questions contemplated in the seminar so that students gain insight into the prompt's charge.

First, let's consider the qualities that make for a clear, purposeful prompt. As you read each criterion in the following list, consider the two prompts below it and ask which one meets the qualities in the criterion.

1. **Is the prompt worth teaching?** You will spend several days on the reading and writing portions of the lesson plan, so choose a topic that allows students to acquire specific skills relevant to the study of the discipline and to subject area and literacy standards. These two samples were written for a middle school science class. Which one best meets this criterion?

   • Is stem cell harvesting a good policy or not? Write an editorial in which you state a position.

- How do cells work together to form tissue and organs? Write a report in which you explain this process and provide examples from your research.

2. **Is the prompt clear, doable, and understandable?** If students can't understand the purpose and demands asked of them, then their work will reflect that. Here are common ways that muddled prompts confuse the writer:

   - The prompt's mode is unclear. For example, *Is Iago a sympathetic character? Write an essay in which you explain Iago as Othello's alter ego.* In this case, it's not clear if students are to write an argumentative or explanatory response.
   - The prompt is not specific enough. For example, *How do the arts shape, as well as reflect, a culture?* A doable prompt sets the stage for a manageable and focused response, whereas this question is more like a unit's essential or overarching theme. An assignment is not a unit. In comparison, an assignment that sits inside a unit focuses on a more specific question: *"What common artistic symbols were used by the Incas and the Mayans?"* (McTighe & Wiggins, 2013, p. 1).
   - The prompt isn't relevant to the discipline. Assignments that teach students content and literacy skills should focus on content. Philosophical or ethical questions such as *Is the death penalty moral?* belong in philosophy class but not in science or history class.
   - The product is unstated or unclear. For example, *Relate how you solved the problem.*
   - The prompt is biased or steers students to a common response. For example, *Write a book report in which you explain why Bigger Thomas in* Native Son *is an antihero.*

3. **If there is a question, is it text-based?** A text-based question relates directly to some element of a text: *How does the author. . . ? What is the meaning of (a word, phrase, passage, act, etc.)? Which*

theory. . . ? Why is the character. . . ? Even if there isn't a question, does the prompt relate to one or more texts as the basis for evidence? The DWC prompt depends on a good or implied question that is explored in the DWC assignment seminar. The following prompt, written by middle school language arts teachers, clearly involves students in a text and aligns to standards for reading in which students examine perspectives and write an argumentative response.

Which point of view is Noyes most sympathetic to? After reading, "The Highwayman" by Alfred Noyes, write a literary critique in which you address the question and argue from whose perspective, Bess's or the Highwayman's, the author most sympathizes. Support your discussion with evidence from the text.

4. **Does the prompt align to a cluster of grade-level standards and their demands?** For example, an 11th grade prompt aligned to Common Core RL.3 should require students to demonstrate their ability to "analyze in detail" elements of a work of literature in more rigorous ways than 7th or 4th grade prompts, but all share a common focus on character, setting, and plot. Can you tell which prompt is written for 4th grade, 7th grade, and 11th? Why or why not? Check your English language arts standards to discern the grade level for these prompts.

    Write an essay in which you determine and analyze the impact of the author's choices in (text) regarding how to develop and relate the elements.

    Write an essay in which you analyze how lines in (text) reveal aspects of the main character.

    Write an essay in which you describe how (character) in (story) responds to major events and challenges.

5. **Does the text work well with the demands and content in the prompt and allow you to teach specific skills and thinking?** A text should stretch students at all levels in some way. The text can be a passage in a novel or a chapter in a science book, an act in a dramatic work, a painting, a recording of a speech, or a data chart.

It does not have to be long, but it needs to have something worth thinking about, as stated in the focus standard. The text is a good way to distinguish the rigor from one grade to another even when the teaching tasks are similar. If your assignment involves researching multiple sources, designate a few sources you know so that you can teach skills necessary for gathering information and citing evidence. You can then allow students to find and research others on their own.

This example of a 9th grade text that stretches students to analyze primary and secondary sources comes from a Rockaway, New York, teacher:

After reading Robert Kennedy's memoir, 13 Days, and researching two news accounts, write an essay in which you evaluate the accuracy of the event as described in Kennedy's memoir, acknowledging where Kennedy leaves out any facts or notable details. Support your discussion with evidence from the text.

6. **Does the prompt set up a manageable instructional plan?** If the prompt is loaded with too many cognitive or writing demands, students will become bogged down during the production process, as you try to teach a long list of skills and they try to manage multiple demands. Eventually, as the lesson drags on, students will lose interest, and so will you. It's better to teach a series of shorter assignments than one long one.

    Consider this example, or try to respond to it. We think you will see that it involves too many topics and doesn't really ask for any connections for students to write concisely and thoughtfully about:

    Write a three-paragraph report in which you discuss the cultural, geographical, and religious traditions of Sudan tribes.

    A revision might be the following:

    Write an essay based on the memoir we read in seminar in which you discuss how the geography of the Sudan has influenced cultural traditions.

Exemplar prompts. The following are examples of prompts that meet the criteria above and set the stage for effective instruction. The prompts were adapted from questions found in national sources, which you can find online and use for your own prompts.

> *Where do you think most of the food in the United States is grown, and how do you know? After studying the landform types on the map, write a report in which you identify at least four landforms and discuss what food products might be grown there and how you know that.* (Elementary School, National Geographic)

> *What do you understand of the characters and the situation in the passage? Write an essay in which you analyze Dill's and Scout's interest in Boo and relate it to the story as a whole. Support your discussion with evidence from the text.* (High School, International Baccalaureate)

> *What are algorithms, and how do we use them every day? Write a response in which you address the question and provide examples.* (Elementary School, Kahn Academy)

> *What does Dickens's* The Old Curiosity Shop *suggest about the power of individual will as compared to the effects of law? After reading and discussing this selection, write an essay in which you analyze the relationship between individual will and the effects of law. Support your discussion with evidence from the text.* (Middle School, National Paideia Center)

Now that you've considered the qualities that make an effective prompt, let's move on to the other elements of an assignment.

Step 7: Write a Rubric (or Select One)

A rubric should not be a checklist of demands but, rather, a detailed description that helps students understand the qualities they must demonstrate in their products. The best rubrics provide at least two levels of performance: "meets expectations" and "advanced." When a rubric and the scoring process are approached as means for providing feedback, they are more useful to students and result in students taking ownership of the process. As Sharrat and Fullan write, schools that label the rubric and scoring process "descriptive feedback" and "success criteria" convey to students that scoring is not about failure and success in silos but about an ongoing and interactive effort to create a trajectory of learning and improvement (2012, pp. 67–75).

Step 8: Test Your Prompt and Rubric

The best way to understand what you are asking your students to do is to try it yourself. As you write, note the cognitive and writing skills you use along the way. These, along with the demands and qualities noted in your prompt and rubric, should become your instructional steps. We repeat: an assignment is taught step by step, and the number and focus of steps depend on the needs of your students and on how much guidance and intervention they may need to acquire a skill and understanding of that step (Dougherty, 2012, p. 67).

After both your prompt and rubric are in place, the next step is to create an instructional plan that will give all of your students the opportunity to be successful.

Step 9: Write an Instructional Plan

After the opening seminar based on the text you've chosen, writing instruction should involve students in some type of discourse strategy, such as small-group conversations, debates, presentations, and class discussions that blend the writing process with speaking and listening activities. Below is a sample DWC plan for grades 4–12 based on 55-minute class times.

- Period 1: Participate in a seminar. Students focus on the text that they will write about in the Writing Sequence.
- Period 2: Deconstruct the prompt and rubric. Ensure that students understand the purpose and charge in the prompt and rubric.
- Period 3: Write a thesis or claim statement and an outline (opening, development, and closing). This is an opportunity to develop students' skills in organizing their thinking.

- Period 4: Write a first draft; begin revision process. Use this step to develop their choice of language, their sentence construction, and transitions from point to point.
- Period 5: Revise and edit for logic, evidence, elaboration, and fluency. Teach students how to elaborate using details and examples, to refine their logic, and to ensure they have relevant evidence.
- Period 6: Format and turn in composition. If applicable, teach students to insert data, graphs, or charts and how to format final copies for publication or their readership.

The purpose of the instructional plan is to provide you with a guide that notes the sequence of instructional events you plan to ensure students produce high-quality products. You might include, for example, actual strategies, such as pair-sharing, along with each teaching event. Developing an instructional plan in collaboration with other teachers is a powerful experience for many teachers. In Fresno, California, middle school disciplinary teachers work together every other week to write instructional plans. During these sessions they help each other develop a sequence of short instructional tasks and share expertise and resources. In Bridgeport, Connecticut, English and science teachers work together on assignments that involve writing about science content. One teacher commented that "This was an opportunity for subject area teacher collaboration that was useful and practical. We have not had much (or any) time this year for true subject area collaboration."

In Part 2, we go into more detail about the teaching of structure and strategies you can use during the writing process.

Step 10: Teach!

Once you have your prompt written, your rubric, and an instructional plan, you are ready to do the most important step in this process—teach the assignment.

A note on formative instruction. We do not go into detail about these final two steps in this book. However, we think it's important to remind you that formative instruction involves continuous reflection on the effectiveness of our instructional choices. True formative instruction occurs when you not only analyze student work for strengths and weaknesses but also act on that analysis to rethink your assignments. In doing so, you monitor the trajectory of learning that occurs in your course.

Josh, an English teacher in Colorado, tells us that he is never satisfied with his assignments and almost always makes adjustments to his prompts or instructional plans, sometimes even as he teaches the assignment. Karen, an elementary teacher in Oregon, teaches six or more assignments each term and says that over the last four years she has "never taught an assignment the same way." If you make adjustments to each assignment and base those adjustments on previous student work products, you should see continuous improvement in your assignments, your instruction, and your students' products.

Step 11: Analyze Student Work Products

Scoring student products is not the same as scoring assessments. You are not looking for summative data—a score to represent student achievement—as much as you are looking for feedback. You should look for trends in the class set and ask questions such as, "What patterns of success do I see?" and "What patterns of student struggle do I see?" This kind of analysis will help you determine what instruction was effective and what was not. It also helps you plan the next assignment so that you know where you may need to reteach some writing skills or "let go" of others as students demonstrate competence and can work independently. For example, if students have mastered paragraphing, you might turn your attention to weaker skills such as teaching them to discern and cite more relevant evidence.

Working collaboratively on crafting assignments and scoring helps build consensus about expectations, and most important, team members can share instructional strategies and resources as they discuss what they see in student products. As one teacher said, "True learning for me would be to go over those lessons as a group and really dive into and critique them." Students also can learn to participate in the scoring process and give useful feedback. One high school student who gave feedback to a classmate reflected that it made her feel "like a teacher." She said looking at his paper helped her see what she should have done in her paper. We have heard students make similar comments many times in our work.

A science teacher told us, "I think it reminded me of the importance of sharing learning both as teachers and students. It was a help to talk with other individuals about what they saw in my lesson and what I saw in their lesson. It also made me realize or think about the importance of having my students come together and talk with each other either in groups or as a whole class about what they had learned from that lesson. I sometimes forget the enrichment that can be gained from having everyone share their insights after the task is done instead of just focusing on what the lesson showed me about each individual student."

Step 12: Revise Your Assignment—And Write a New One

At this point, you should revise the assignment's prompt or instructional plan to improve it using student work feedback from your analysis. You are also ready to craft a new assignment. This new assignment takes its cue from lessons learned from the last assignment and should incorporate skills that need reteaching and introduce new ones.

Once you have finalized your DWC assignment prompt and instructional plan, you are ready to lead your students through the discourse and writing sequences in a way that provides them with the opportunity and motivation to succeed. One of the best ways we have found working with teachers is to craft and teach assignments together. That challenge brings us to the core of this book—the use of discourse to inspire writing. In the chapters that follow, we will explore in detail how to teach using classroom discussion to enhance the writing stage, thereby making the ideas that shape your curriculum accessible to all your students.

CHECK YOUR THINKING

Consider the following two prompts and compare their clarity and purpose. Try writing the opening paragraph for each prompt. Are the prompts clear and doable?

A. After reading *Johnny Tremain*, write an essay in which you compare the Lyte family to the Lorne family and explain how they help the reader understand a historical context. Support your discussion with evidence from the text.

B. Why do we need society? Discuss how the characters and the theme are related in *Lord of the Flies*.

See Appendix C (p. 162) for possible responses.

Figure 2.1

DWC Assignment Steps

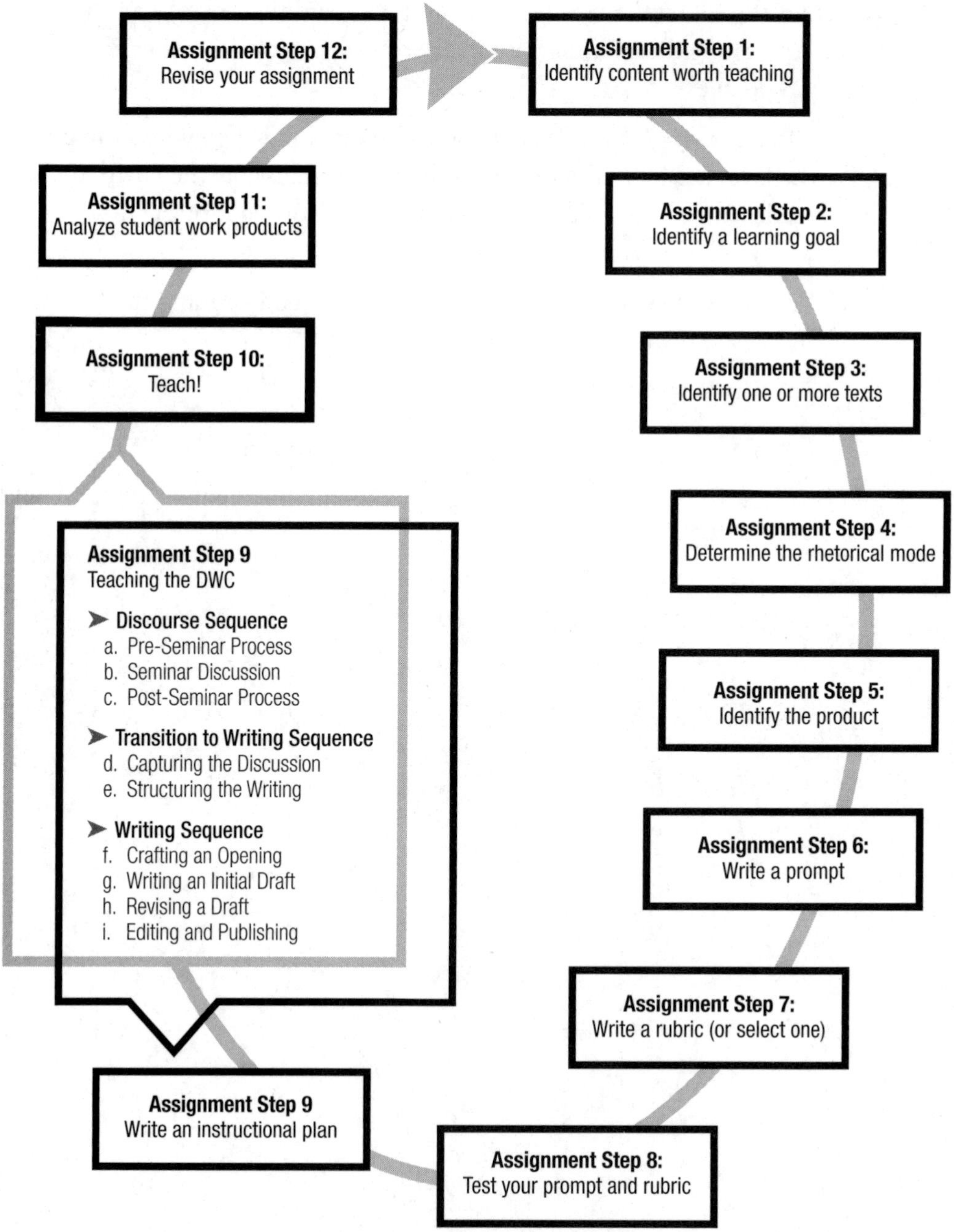

Assignment Step 12:
Revise your assignment

Assignment Step 1:
Identify content worth teaching

Assignment Step 11:
Analyze student work products

Assignment Step 2:
Identify a learning goal

Assignment Step 10:
Teach!

Assignment Step 3:
Identify one or more texts

Assignment Step 9
Teaching the DWC

➤ **Discourse Sequence**
   a. Pre-Seminar Process
   b. Seminar Discussion
   c. Post-Seminar Process

➤ **Transition to Writing Sequence**
   d. Capturing the Discussion
   e. Structuring the Writing

➤ **Writing Sequence**
   f. Crafting an Opening
   g. Writing an Initial Draft
   h. Revising a Draft
   i. Editing and Publishing

Assignment Step 4:
Determine the rhetorical mode

Assignment Step 5:
Identify the product

Assignment Step 6:
Write a prompt

Assignment Step 7:
Write a rubric (or select one)

Assignment Step 9
Write an instructional plan

Assignment Step 8:
Test your prompt and rubric

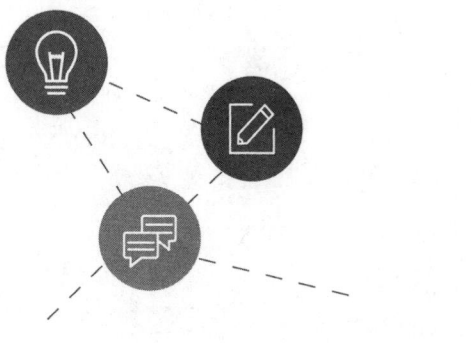

From Discourse
to Writing

In Part 1, you were introduced to the Discourse and Writing Cycle, and we outlined a multistep process for writing an effective DWC assignment (see Figure 2.1). The assignment itself consists of three sequences that we will explore in Part 2: the Discourse Sequence (Chapter 3), the Transition to Writing Sequence (Chapter 4), and the Writing Sequence (Chapter 5). Chapter 6 gives an in-depth example of the fully realized cycle in an 8th grade science class.

3

Discourse: Thinking Out Loud

The most fruitful and natural exercise of the mind, in my opinion, is conversation.

—Michael de Montaigne, *The Essays of Michel Eyquem de Montaigne*

In this chapter, we discuss a method of discourse appropriate for all students of any age or ability. The Discourse Sequence, the first part of the Discourse and Writing Cycle, is the key to inspiring students to write. Its purpose is to engage students in communal conversation about the ideas and information in a shared text and to exercise speaking and listening skills in preparation for the writing component of the assignment. Students participate in this discussion format—the Paideia seminar—which allows them to explore ideas, develop language, and build those skills in fluency and elaboration that they need to produce quality written products in their academic subjects.

Even before the Discourse Sequence begins, students should have completed multiple, close readings and studied the vocabulary contained in the text, which they will then discuss and write about in detail. Indeed, the model lesson plans contained in Chapter 10 stress the pre-seminar content reading that should occur prior to the DWC. However, since our focus in this book is on how discourse inspires writing, we begin here with seminar discourse.

USING SEMINARS TO INSPIRE THINKING AND WRITING

The structure of classroom discussion detailed in this chapter is a specific version of Socratic discourse called a Paideia seminar. In our experience, it is the most productive form of whole-class discourse: "a collaborative, intellectual discourse facilitated with open-ended questions about a text" (Roberts & Billings, 2003, p. 16). The Paideia seminar has a clear structure and process that systematizes the three characteristics of successful classroom discussion described later in this chapter. When conducted with these features in mind, Paideia seminars are

- **Collaborative.** Participants cooperate intellectually rather than compete, building on each other's thoughts to construct more sophisticated understandings of the ideas under discussion.
- **Intellectual.** Participants address ideas and values, not factual information, and so struggle with the ambiguity presented by challenging concepts.
- **Democratic.** Participants engage by sharing their thoughts, through both statements and questions, and everyone's response has equal weight.
- **Open-ended.** The teacher leads the seminar by asking questions that have multiple "right" answers, thereby evoking a wide variety of responses from a wide variety of participants.
- **Text-driven.** The seminar is anchored by a text, which is a human artifact that embodies the curricular ideas and values chosen by the teacher.

The goal of a text-based Paideia seminar is for students to practice their thinking, both individually and collectively, about a series of ideas. For example, in a social studies unit focused on the ideas of justice, equality, and responsibility, the Paideia seminar text might be the "Universal Declaration of Human Rights." Students grapple with the reading of a complex text, both to learn vocabulary and to see how their ideas about justice compare to those of thinkers in other eras.

Because of the intimate relationship between thoughts and words, the students simultaneously develop their fluency as well as their understanding of key ideas. Well-managed and -directed, the students' growing ability to articulate their thoughts carries over into their writing. Because of the seminar, the same students who could do little more than shrug expressively when originally faced with the text now find that they are armed with both ideas and the language to express those ideas. See Chapter 10 for a full range of sample Paideia seminar plans that embody the Discourse and Writing Cycle.

DISCOURSE SEQUENCE

The Discourse Sequence involves three stages:

- Pre-Seminar Process
- Seminar Discussion
- Post-Seminar Process

Teaching through whole-group discussion is a natural classroom routine. However, teachers often talk far too much when they lead whole-class discussion, causing students' attention to quickly fade. Developing lesson plans for whole-class discussion and setting the right conditions can create meaningful interactions that challenge student thinking. We have seen many teachers successfully build whole-group discussion routines by attending to the three important steps included in this sequence: pre-seminar process activities, the seminar discussion itself, and post-seminar process reflection and assessment. We'll describe each of these three steps in detail to illustrate how, across grade levels and subject areas, students can fully participate in the collaborative thinking that leads to quality writing.

Pre-Seminar Process

In this first essential step of the Discourse Sequence, the teacher sets the stage for the discussion by clearly defining and introducing the seminar process, regardless of how many times the students have participated before. The teacher-facilitator then leads a detailed discussion of her own roles and responsibilities as well as those of the student-participants. This ritualistic opening of every Discourse Sequence helps set the stage for truly civil dialogue.

Once the roles and responsibilities are clear, then a brief period of formative self-assessment occurs. The teacher deliberately invites students to reflect on their own personal habits for speaking and listening and to identify and commit (in writing) to personal participation goals. When we were asked to create a rubric for speaking and listening aligned with the Common Core Anchor Standards for those skills, we identified the following categories: *attention, engagement, articulation, explanation, expansion,* and *connection* (see Figure 3.1). Based on knowledge of students' strengths and experience, the teacher can break these down into discrete behaviors that demonstrate mastery of specific speaking and listening skills. For example, a reticent student may select "speak voluntarily two times" as a personal articulation goal. Similarly, a talkative student may decide to work on "referring to the text at least once," an explanation goal.

In addition to individual participation goals, the teacher either assigns or facilitates agreement on a group discussion goal. For example, with young students and groups just beginning the process, a group goal may be "look at the person speaking" (attention) or "give way if you start talking the same time someone else does" (connection). Ideally, the group goal is displayed prominently so that everyone can refer to it throughout the discussion.

Seminar Discussion

The teacher facilitates the discussion itself by asking clear, open-ended questions. These planned questions center around the ideas and values embedded in the text and give shape (a beginning, middle, and end) to the discussion (see Figure 3.2).

The first question in any good discussion is designed to have the students identify the most intriguing aspects of the text and lure all the

Figure 3.1

Paideia Seminar Speaking and Listening Rubric

Demands and Qualities	Not Yet	Proficient	Advanced
Attention	• Does not look at the person speaking • Occasionally turns and talks to person sitting nearby while another person is speaking	• Looks at the person speaking during most of the discussion • Rarely talks while another is speaking	• Looks at the person speaking during the discussion • Does not talk while another is speaking
Engagement	• Does not take notes related to the ideas being discussed	• Occasionally takes notes related to the ideas being discussed • Gives way to another as a way of sharing the talk time	• Consistently takes notes related to the ideas being discussed • Gives way to another as a way of sharing the talk time
Articulation	• Makes barely audible statements	• Makes clear and accurate statements; generally speaks at appropriate pace, volume; uses relevant vocabulary and grammar	• Makes clear and accurate statements; consistently speaks at appropriate pace, volume; uses relevant vocabulary and grammar
Explanation (Justification)	• Makes simple, somewhat unrelated or repetitive points/statements	• Provides points/statements about the discussion topic noting details related to sequence, category, purpose, or point of view • Refers to the text or another relevant source	• Provides insight related to fallacies within the text; tests assumptions and explores inferences • Refers to the text or another relevant source

continued

Figure 3.1

Paideia Seminar Speaking and Listening Rubric (*continued*)

Demands and Qualities	Not Yet	Proficient	Advanced
Expansion	• Draws conclusions based on a single perspective	• Considers another point of view and states personal bias	• Illuminates relevance; notes positive/negative implications • Acknowledges difference in own perspectives—before and now • Adds to previous statement by offering a more global/ holistic interpretation
Connection	• Does not ask questions • Does not refer to what else has been said	• Asks authentic questions • Paraphrases what else has been said	• Refers to another facet of an idea or another's comment • Considers multiple points of view while acknowledging personal bias • Asks authentic, thought-provoking, open-ended questions

participants into the discussion from the beginning. For example, an opening question about the Cherokee folktale "How the Terrapin Beat the Rabbit" might be, "Which character could you defend? And why?" If the text is Martin Luther King Jr.'s speech "I Have a Dream," the opening question might be, "Which is the most important paragraph? And why?" An effective opening question is often asked in two parts that require two different types of response: the first part through a round-robin reply and the second part through spontaneous sharing. In other words, all the students are expected to share their concise responses to the first part of the question in turn, allowing everyone to join in the discussion. The second part of the question allows individuals to speak spontaneously and in a

Figure 3.2

Seminar Question Sequence

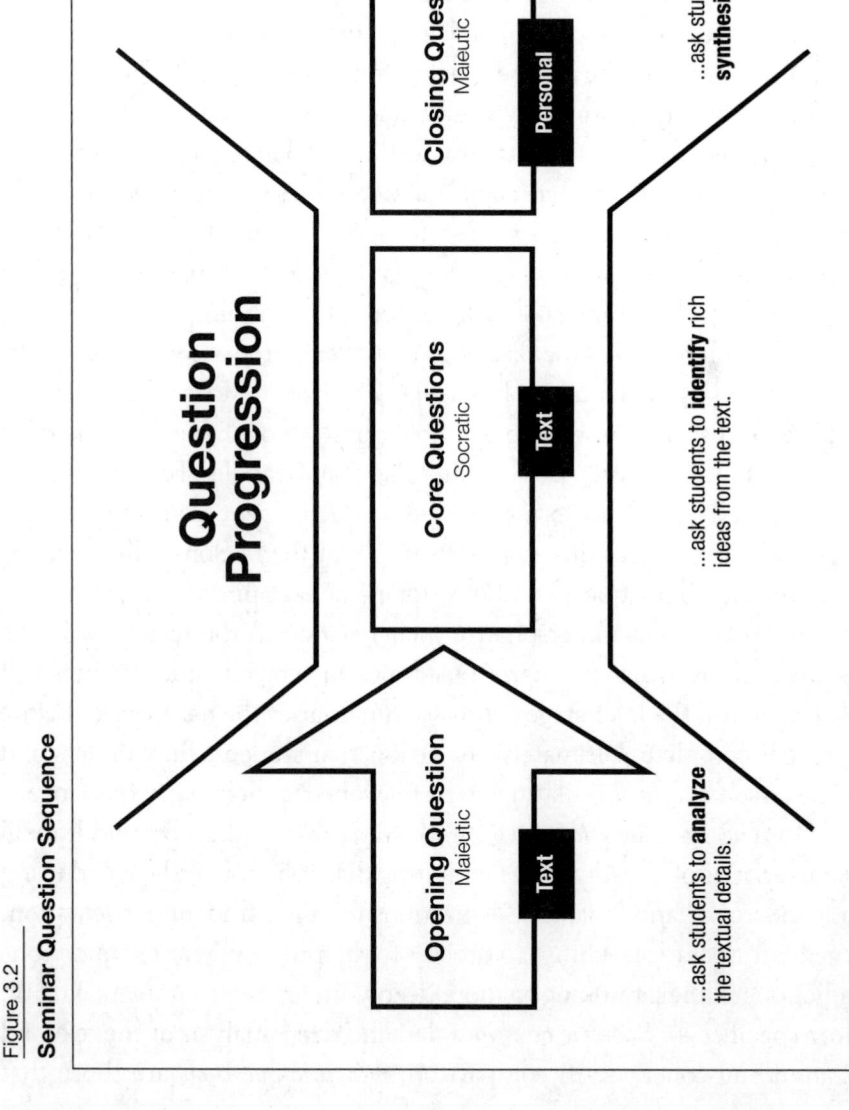

way that connects ideas. Notice the first question requires only a basic level of comprehension in order to reply so that participants can feel safe taking this first step. Yet it's also open-ended and invites all participants into the discussion.

The middle section of the discussion is framed by what we call core questions. *Core questions* require students to analyze the details of the text. A sample core question on the Pledge of Allegiance might be, "What did the author mean by the phrase 'one nation under God?'" The cognitive demand of these questions is typically much greater than that of the opening questions, forcing students to wrestle with language, structure, and intent in the text. Because core questions require students to delve deeply into the text, a teacher may choose to have students think silently and reread closely, do a short bit of writing, or have a short, paired discussion to give them the time and space for deeper understanding.

Toward the end of the discussion, the facilitator poses a *closing question* that asks students to apply and personalize the ideas from the text and the discussion. For example, a final question on "The Star-Spangled Banner" could be, "Why do we sing 'The Star-Spangled Banner' at public events today?" Or a closing question on a segment from *Frankenstein* might be, "What does this story tells us about the responsibility of a scientist today?" This question allows for personal opinion and reflection. Students often want to personalize their reaction to the text early in the discussion, but a wise facilitator postpones the consideration of personal relevance until the later stages of the seminar, after the hard work of close reading is complete. Ultimately, the goal is that students fully understand the text itself before speculating on its relevance to their own experience.

In *The Paideia Proposal* (1982), Mortimer Adler notes additional characteristics of questions for facilitating discussion. He advocated using both "Socratic" and "maieutic" questions to guide student participation. In general, Socratic teaching is a process for helping students examine contradictions in their thinking to more deeply understand a universal truth. More specifically, *Socratic questions* demand deep analysis of the text and its attending concepts. In comparison, *maieutic questions* are those that help students recognize and articulate their own truth. *Maieutic* comes from the same root as *midwifery* and means to help another give birth, in this instance, to their ideas. In short, Socratic questions are about universal truth, and maieutic questions are about individual truths.

"What is the most important phrase in the Declaration of Independence?" is a maieutic question. Participants may choose among all the sentences in the document and provide their individual rationale for the selection. Although the text serves as the foundation for student response, this question honors individual choice and interpretation. In contrast, "What does Jefferson mean by 'Life, Liberty and the pursuit of Happiness'?" is a more Socratic question. These words were deliberately selected to convey values of the newly developed democratic government. Socratic questions help students develop the standard readings of texts. Experienced facilitators combine Socratic and maieutic questions in order to honor both individual students and the text. In this way, the Socratic questions help with the close reading, and the maieutic questions engage students in a way that draws on their personal experience.

When we overlay the distinction between maieutic and Socratic queries with the sequence of opening, core, and closing questions, we find that asking a maieutic question to start, followed by several Socratic questions, works well to engage the students in an increasingly sophisticated discussion. After doing the deep textual analysis required by Socratic core questions, the closing, more maieutic question allows students to think about and discuss how the ideas and values in the text are relevant in their own lives.

This sequence of opening, core, and closing questions repeated in discussion after discussion creates a valuable classroom ritual. The predictability helps students think deeply and feel safe in sharing their thoughts. Student engagement leads to genuine insight as participants see the connections between course content and their own, larger world.

Teachers should draft and carefully revise all of these questions beforehand. Yet the facilitator may also need to ask spontaneous, follow-up questions during the discussion. In that case, be mindful that the follow-up questions are not asked merely to test or challenge students but, rather, to help them clarify their thinking about the text or what has been said. The facilitator's job is to help students learn **how** to think, not necessarily **what** to think.

Post-Seminar Process

After the seminar discussion and before the end of the period, students are given time to reflect on their goals and their participation during this particular discussion. Students complete a short written self-assessment, and then the teacher leads the group in a brief oral assessment of the group goal. (Be careful here not to allow evaluative comments by one student about another. This group assessment should remain focused on the group, not individuals.) We suggest the teacher take notes on the group's progress as a way of preparing for the next formal discussion. Similarly, when students make notes about their individual participation and use them to prepare for the next seminar, the continuity between discussions sets a healthy climate of self-awareness and growth. Students' development as speakers and listeners can be accurately documented through self-assessment. In this way assessment is closely related to the individuals taking responsibility for the development of their own skills.

Keep in mind that assessment of productive discourse illuminates what good conversationalists do, much like a "think aloud" uncovers what skilled thinkers do. This kind of reflection on communication skills can help students move beyond personality and gender habits as well as cultural expectations. The point is to honor individuality while challenging all to practice their discussion skills and clarify their thinking.

This format for whole-class discussion invites students to participate in ways other class activities do not. Structured, whole-class discussion is most useful when designed to authentically include students and help them practice articulating their ideas while substantiating their perspective with credible evidence. Practicing collaborative, intellectual discourse may be one of the most meaningful learning experiences a student can enjoy in a day. Likewise, we as teachers are often surprised and amused by what students share. For those of us who believe in the importance of open-mindedness, it is truly music to our ears when during class discourse, a student says

"I've changed my mind. . . ." This is genuine, intellectual learning. Further-more, whole-class discussion can be a profoundly unifying experience that strengthens the sense of community within the classroom.

WHEN DO YOU USE THE PAIDEIA SEMINAR?

We recommend the establishment of whole-class discussion as an instruc-tional *ritual,* to be used consistently and often as an introduction to writing. If students participate in the same type of formal discourse several times a month, they learn to trust both the process and the teacher. Furthermore, they learn the habits of mind consistent with collaborative inquiry, which leads to genuine understanding. When you plan your own unit or course, set a goal of holding classroom discussions often enough so that students can develop these important skills—speaking, listening, thinking—as a natural part of classroom life.

The Paideia seminar fits well into a writing-intensive unit in at least three places. The first is at the beginning of a unit, when the seminar serves as an introduction to a text and a set of ideas. If a middle school social studies teacher wanted to teach a writing-intensive unit on freedom, citizenship, and civil rights, she might start the unit with a seminar on the Pledge of Allegiance, wherein the students consider the ideas of country, freedom, and loyalty.

The second opportunity for a Paideia seminar is in the middle of a unit of study, after a close reading of the text and before the writing pro-cess itself. This is a common location in a writing-based unit, because the close and extensive reading of the text prepares all students to participate in the seminar. For example, if the unit theme is focused on equity, language, and relationships, the seminar text might be the Gettysburg Address. The ideas and language that are generated during the seminar then feed directly into the students' writing. Placing the seminar in the middle of the cycle of instruction means that you can scaffold student reading of a chal-lenging text, so that all the students will be better prepared to discuss it in detail. You can then build in a Transition to Writing stage (see Chapter 4) immediately following the seminar, wherein your students make notes on everything they said or heard during the seminar that applies to the writing task. Middle school literacy facilitator Melissa Hedt stresses the value of seminar discussion prior to writing because the "seminar empowers our reluctant writers by giving them the raw material—both words and ideas—with which to begin the writing process."

The third point when a Paideia seminar yields rewards is after the final drafts of the student papers are finished and published. A Paideia seminar at this point in the cycle of instruction serves as a capstone discourse in which students can bring to the seminar circle all of the insights they generated during the DWC. If students have reflected at each stage in the unit on how their thinking has evolved, then they will be intellectually primed for a powerful seminar by all that they learned through the process. For example, the writing assignment in a unit on immigration might be the following:

> *What should citizenship in our country be based on? After reading and discussing "The New Colossus," write a letter to Congress arguing for guiding principles in making new immigration laws. Refer to the text as well as other relevant sources.*

The whole-class discourse at the end of a unit based on this assignment helps students synthesize ideas and see connections between readings.

Each of these three points in the instructional cycle has advantages for a Paideia seminar; however, the seminar probably influences writing most significantly when it occurs between a close reading of a text (including careful vocabulary study) and the initiation of the writing process—where the insights generated during the seminar will lead directly to student writing that is more clear, coherent, and sophisticated.

CHECK YOUR THINKING

How do you see seminars fitting into a unit of study in your classroom?

See Appendix C (p. 162) for possible responses.

4

Transition: Preparing to Write

Bad thinking can never lead to good writing.
—Teacher quoted in *Teaching Writing* (McDonald & McDonald, 2002)

At this point in the Discourse and Writing Cycle, students have done a lot of thinking—both about the text and about the ideas and values embedded in the text. All of this thinking does your students little good, however, unless they can recall it later during the various stages of the writing process. The transition from the discourse in the Paideia seminar to writing in the classroom—the subject of this chapter—is primarily a matter of gleaning and organizing. The strategies in this chapter are designed to help students transfer the new ideas and new language they just experienced into resources they can draw on while writing.

Here we focus on instruction that will help your students gather evidence and develop an outline. In the next chapter we discuss how to guide students through the process of transforming thoughts and notes into prose.

THE TRANSITION TO WRITING SEQUENCE

The Transition to Writing Sequence involves two stages:

- Capturing the Discussion
- Structuring the Writing

In this sequence, students should first analyze the prompt and rubric to make sure they understand the assignment. They should record all of the ideas they thought, heard, or expressed during the seminar—and the language that was used to express those ideas. Then they are ready to create a design for the overall organization of the essay they plan to write.

Students need to be clear about what you want them to do and what is expected of them. Here are some activities teachers can use to ensure students understand the prompt's charge:

- Ask students to circle verbs and discuss what the words mean in small or large groups.
- Ask students to analyze the prompt for audience and purpose. Discuss how these two features impact writing choices in language, tone, and format.
- Ask students what mode the prompt requires. Use this discussion to talk about the differences between argumentation and explanatory or informational writing or between opinion and argumentation. Change the prompt so that it reads in both modes and ask students to articulate how, as authors, they would adjust their language and tone.
- As a class, identify and chart the features of a professional piece of writing that are similar to the product in your prompt.
- Ask students to identify one or more qualities in the rubric's criteria they will aspire to demonstrate in their final compositions. Discuss their meanings, and ask students to find examples in professional writing. Weight these criteria when you score.

Once students understand the charge in the writing assignment prompt and rubric, you should move on to the next two instructional stages in the Transition to Writing Sequence.

Capturing the Discussion

Capturing the discussion involves teaching students to record on paper the language and ideas from the discussion. Ideally, you should ask your students to do this as soon after the seminar as possible. Here are four interrelated steps that you can follow, using some or all of these strategies depending on how much scaffolding your students need. Note that the first two steps can be completed as "two-column notes" for later comparison.

1. **List significant ideas heard, said, or thought during the seminar.** Ask students to list at random any insights (large or small) that they heard, said, or thought during the seminar discussion. Stress that this is an initial, rough list and not to worry about spelling or grammar. The idea is to grab as many ideas as possible without worrying about their relative significance.

2. **List significant words, phrases, or sentences that seem to capture these thoughts effectively.** Note that this is a slightly different assignment than the first step because this is about the language used during the discussion. Stress that students should also copy into their lists (using quotation marks) or highlight in the text any passages that took on particular significance. Further, they should link in their notes language from the text with language they generated themselves where appropriate.

3. **Compare the lists of significant ideas and language to the writing prompt.** Once students have recorded both the ideas and language from the seminar discussion, display the writing task again and discuss it further as needed. Then ask the students to go through the text and the notes they recorded in the first two steps above, highlighting the elements that could potentially help them respond to the prompt. A further step is to have them create a new

and more refined set of notes that captures the raw material from the text and the discussion that is most relevant to the prompt.

4. **Write a temporary controlling idea.** At this point in the process, students may have some idea of what they want to say in response to the prompt, so have them write a temporary statement as a claim or thesis, depending on the mode of your prompt. Then have them note the relationships between the ideas and language they recorded in the first three steps and this temporary thesis.

The last two steps described above are preparing students to cite evidence in support of their eventual claim or thesis. Citing evidence begins with filtering out what's not relevant and identifying what is relevant to an assignment. It involves the sorting and selecting that creates the feature called "relevance" and "precision" in rubrics. Note that as students gather evidence, they often get an emerging sense of what the composition can address—and sometimes what it cannot. They might find that a claim or thesis doesn't hold up but that some other aspect or point of view does. Encourage students to continue refining and revising their temporary claims or theses throughout the outlining and drafting stages.

Structuring the Writing

This stage involves helping students organize what are still relatively random ideas into a line of thought as they move toward composing a first draft. Whatever format you use, the best method for planning an essay is the creation of an outline—the more detailed, the better. Experienced writing teachers consider this the most important stage in successful writing. As one history teacher emphasized, "I spend a lot of teaching time on outlining because I know if my students have a good structure to work with, they will be able to stay focused on the process of writing while composing their essays."

In elementary or middle school classrooms, paragraphs are sufficient to serve as the structural components of a composition. Later, in high school, students can structure longer compositions in terms of sections, which contain one or more paragraphs, in order to provide a more elaborated argument or explanation. All formal structures involve at least three sections: an opening, a main body, and a closing. Variations on structures are determined by the mode and cognitive charge, usually flagged by verbs, in an assignment. For example, an assignment in which students define and explain a concept would entail *at least* four paragraphs: an opening paragraph, a main body that includes a definition paragraph and an explanatory paragraph, and a closing paragraph. An assignment in which students take a position would follow the basic three-part structure, but the main body might involve more than one reason and, therefore, more than one paragraph. Students can become aware of how writers' structure works if you have them study text structures during reading lessons. In order to structure a composition, students need to settle on a claim or thesis. This is the time to revise any temporary statements, if students wrote them earlier.

Outlining as thinking. Successful writing teachers know that outlining prevents straggling prose and weak connections within a composition. Because students must organize their work and give it shape, outlining forces students to go deeper in their thought processes as they sort through the facts and ideas in their notes and in their heads. Outlining in some form is the first stage in delineating a line of thought. Experienced writing teachers spend more time on this stage than any other. They typically provide students with templates and conference with each student to ensure they have defined the structure and line of thought appropriate for the assignment. Spending time and effort on this stage provides an opportunity to teach thinking about ordering ideas and supporting those ideas. This instruction makes the difference between loosely connected pieces of evidence and ones that closely illustrate or support the main idea of each paragraph and the composition as a whole. One experienced writing teacher told us that outlining is her "main defense against chaos."

Here are several different forms of outlining that you can choose from depending on the skill and experience of your students:

1. **Traditional outlining.** This is the 1.A.a. version of an outline. Most grammar textbooks have examples of traditional outlines, and there are software programs that guide students through this format. Ask students to first sort the ideas (and language) they gleaned from the text and discussion into logical groupings in a logical sequence.

2. **Sentence outlining.** Ask students to write a set of topic sentences that capture their most important points or reasons. Have them work in pairs to rearrange these sentences, perhaps chronologically or from most to least important. Work with them to eliminate any irrelevant sentences and replace them with relevant ones.

3. **Blueprinting.** Provide students with a template that consists of a number of rectangular boxes as a visual guide for structuring the sections of their compositions. Each box stands for a section, not necessarily a paragraph. The simplest template consists of three boxes: one for an opening, one for development, and one for closure. A more specific outline includes boxes for each of the paragraphs within the three sections. For example, an assignment prompt that asks for students to compare two characters would probably have at least two sections in the development space of the template. Once these sections are established, students should break them down into paragraph-sized segments using bullets or another strategy so that they have a more detailed record of the ideas within the sections.

4. **Sequencing.** A number of methods involve sequencing, such as storyboarding and timelines. If students are writing an account or a feature article about some event, then this form of outlining is helpful. Using file cards helps students plot their points and experiment with different orders, say, from the first event to the last, or from the most important point to the least or vice versa. This activity makes for fun discussions when students work in pairs or small groups.

The goal of this kind of detailed design work is to plan each paragraph within the composition, no matter how long it is. Within the space for each paragraph, students should compose a topic sentence and list the details they plan to use in support of that topic sentence, including direct references to the texts about which they are writing. In addition, they can list quotes and note specific words or phrases they want to employ in representing their ideas. Ultimately, when the time comes to translate this design into a first draft, the students will be able to focus on writing clear, coherent sentences, as they have already established the order of their thoughts and supporting details.

When your students have completed an initial draft, they are two-thirds of the way through the DWC, and they are ready to begin what was traditionally thought of as "writing," putting sentences on paper more or less in the order they will appear in the final composition. The difference is that they are much more prepared than they would have been in a traditional classroom. During the Discourse Sequence, they generated a rich supply of ideas about the text and language with which to express those ideas; during the first stage of the Transition to Writing Sequence, they captured this raw material and organized their ideas in support of a thesis and their evidence in support of their ideas; and during the second stage of the Transition to Writing Sequence, they structured the piece of writing that will contain all of these ideas and details so that the sections and paragraphs are clear. What is left to do is critical, however. It involves the hard work of refining their thinking and producing clear, coherent prose.

CHECK YOUR THINKING

What makes the outlining stage so important? How might you leverage this practice to teach thinking?

See Appendix C (p. 162) for possible responses.

5

Writing: Refining Ideas for Purpose and Audience

Writing organizes and clarifies our thoughts. Writing is how we think our way into a subject and make it our own. Writing enables us to find out what we know—and what we don't know—about whatever we're trying to learn.

—William Zinsser, *Writing to Learn*

At this stage in the Discourse and Writing Cycle, students are ready to transform their thinking in the form of notes and outlines into prose. To help students make this transformation, you need to coach students' skill development in paragraph development and sentence fluency. During the next stages, students are constructing meaning in a way that is more clear and precise than in discussion. They are taking the ideas and language generated during the Discourse and Transition to Writing Sequences and shaping them into clear, coherent paragraphs. In this chapter we use a sequence common to the traditional writing process. What we add is the use of discourse to develop skills in fluency and elaboration throughout the DWC.

If at this point students are clear about what they want to say, how they are going to structure their compositions, and what evidence they will use to support their controlling ideas, they can move through the drafting stages with greater ease. This allows you to concentrate on important qualities in their prose: usage, accuracy, precision, and coherence. In addition, it's important to remember that even though you used whole-class discourse to set the stage for writing, your students can still benefit from the opportunity to work together throughout the Writing Sequence. As you will see, students continue to learn from each other, especially at the revising and editing stages, when they need each other as readers and editors to help make their writing as strong and clear as possible. Speaking and listening remain important all the way through to the final draft.

SCAFFOLDING STUDENT THINKING

Expository writing presents opportunities for students to engage in the kinds of thinking in which they inquire, examine, and reason. When students understand a difficult concept because they have read about it, examined it, and written about it, their understanding enriches their academic lives and fuels their intellectual growth. For example, one elementary student articulated this connection among discourse, writing, and thinking after writing a reflection paper based on a seminar about "Thorn Rose, the Sleeping Beauty." She stated that she learned what "fate" means and what such stories can teach us about making choices.

To ignite this kind of intellectual energy in your students, make these drafting stages manageable. Focus on only two or three writing skills at a time so that students aren't overwhelmed by the production of a composition. That level of focus will also allow you and your students to concentrate more on critical-thinking skills. Over time, you can add skills as students master previous ones. For example, in the fall you might keep the assignment straightforward and focus instruction on writing a thesis or claim and structuring a less complex composition. Likewise, you can focus on the thinking skills involved in being concise or drawing the reader into the context of the topic. Later in the year, you could add demands in which students must compare two theories and devise a more complex written structure in doing so. Build toward more complex writing assignments as the year progresses, and your students will reach a skill level at which they can manage multiple writing and thinking demands.

As students gain competence, teachers need to stretch students' thinking and writing skills by adding new demands, based on grade-level standards. Other factors that can stretch students' thinking and writing include creating prompts for different audiences, products, and purposes. Consider the following three examples. Each uses the same content but changes the demands by changing the mode, audience, or purpose:

- Examine and discuss in the seminar the mural *Guernica* by Picasso. Write an essay in which you explain how he achieves a sense of harmony and disharmony. Be sure to refer to elements of the painting to support your discussion.
- Examine and discuss Picasso's mural in the seminar. Write an article for the school paper in which you explain the historical context for the mural. Be sure to refer to elements of the painting to support your discussion.
- Would you agree with the art historian who says that Picasso paints with geometry? After participating in a seminar, write a blog post for the school gallery in which you explain your position and your reasons. Be sure to refer to the elements of the painting to support your discussion.

Changing the mode, audience, and purpose of a prompt is a strategy for adding challenge in a prompt. Another way is to bring the grade-level language of the standards into the prompt. However, the surest indicator that students are meeting increasing demands is their progress in elaborating in their compositions. For example, you might track their growth in their abilities to use language that is relevant and precise or to employ more sophisticated reasoning with each new assignment. That is, both a 10th grader and a 5th grader can write a report about metamorphosis in animal life, but you should expect the 10th grader's paper to elaborate more on the details of the topic.

We concluded Chapter 1 with a chart to help visualize the connections among thinking, writing, and the use of classroom discourse. The modified chart in Figure 5.1 shows in bold type new demands that can be added to stretch students' thinking and writing skills. The thinking and writing skills in this chart refer to the Common Core Anchor Standards but are relevant to any writing challenge. Remember to articulate these new demands in your rubric.

TALKING IS NOT WRITING

One of the main challenges inherent in teaching writing is that language in writing differs from speech. The mental transformation from speaking or talking to writing is often hard for students when writing compositions. In fact, it's hard for all writers. The rule of thumb is that the more technical or academic the audience, the more formal the language, format, and tone. The more public the audience is by group or age, the more informal or conversational the product is in language and tone. On a scale from formal to informal writing, the academic essay and technical reports in science are the most formal, while memoirs and letters are the most informal.

Although talking about a topic is essential for developing many of the thinking skills involved in producing coherent prose, students need to recognize that spoken language is not the same as written language. As Janet Emig (1977) noted in the quote at the beginning of Chapter 2, writing is a unique language process, and unlike talking, writing imposes an artificial structure that has to be learned. Your instruction, then, needs to move back and forth between these two language structures. Periodic discussion, whether in small-group, paired, or whole-group scenarios, can help students bridge the gap between the ideas in their heads or notes and the ones they want to express on paper, especially as they struggle to make their written expression more clear and coherent. But in the end, their writing needs to be structured differently than their speech.

Figure 5.1

DWC Thinking Demands and Writing Skills—Expanded

Thinking Skills	DWC Stage	Writing Skills
Distinguish **a range of** textual evidence that is appropriate for the assignment; **analyze a text that is more complex in terms of lexicon, information, or ideas.**	Capturing the Discussion	Read **multiple texts** explicitly; skim and scan; use annotation and note-taking methods; **analyze a text with multiple ideas or explanations.**
Determine and sequence a line of thought or logic to develop explanation or argument; **address different perspectives or competing ideas; compare or analyze in detail.**	Structuring the Writing	Outline a **complex** structure **with sections** using a method that sequences points or reasons.
Determine a credible claim or thesis; frame a relevant **and detailed** context for composition.	Crafting an Opening	Write a credible claim or thesis; **use multiple sections to** provide relevant context.
Link points or ideas; connect relevant examples or citations to controlling idea; **acknowledge and compare alternate POVs.**	Writing an Initial Draft	Construct a multiparagraph composition with an opening, development, and closing; use quotes, citations; **use structural and logic strategies to develop line of thought.**
Check for logic, explanations, or reasoning **by adding details;** ensure statements are accurate and **nuanced; choose and manage language to convey thoughts with precision;** articulate a coherent line of thought.	Revising a Draft	Apply techniques to improve sentence fluency, language usage, logic, and use of supporting material; **apply disciplinary vocabulary or language appropriate to an audience or context.**
Employ grammar and conventions to create **more precise** meanings.	Editing and Publishing	Use correct spelling, punctuation, **and conventions;** use correct citation formats; apply discipline-based protocols; present composition in a readable format; **insert graphs or other tables.**

THE WRITING SEQUENCE

There are four stages in the Writing Sequence:

- Crafting an Opening
- Writing an Initial Draft
- Revising a Draft
- Editing and Publishing

Crafting an Opening

The opening paragraph (or paragraphs) of any composition tells readers why they are reading a work and what to expect. It states the essential points of the discourse that follows and provides the reader with a controlling idea, either a claim or a thesis. (By definition, argumentative essays begin with a claim; explanatory essays begin with a thesis.) Readers also get a preview of the structure of the composition and its parts, whether the writer is defining and explaining some concept, elaborating on a process, or arguing a cause. Experienced writing teachers are often willing to invest more time at this stage in the writing process because, as one teacher describes it, "if you get the introduction right, then the rest of the essay comes much more easily."

    Statement of idea. Before students write an opening paragraph, make sure they have decided on a controlling idea statement—either a claim for an argument or a thesis for an informative or explanatory composition. The claim or thesis is vital because students will be held accountable for supporting it throughout the composition to follow. If you had students write a temporary claim or thesis in the Transition to Writing Sequence, ask them to revise or write new ones if necessary. Their statements, usually one or two sentences, will be inserted into the opening paragraph. At this point in the process, it's a good idea to post everyone's statements next to the assignment prompt and rubric so that students can see how others are thinking about the prompt's charge and make any changes in their own statements they think necessary. Here are three strategies for working through this stage:

- Ask all students to state their controlling idea out loud and explain the rationale.
- If the text presents an argument, have students role-play each side and argue in their own words and quote from the text.
- In pairs, have students listen to each other's controlling idea and restate it another way to check for clarity and give the speaker an alternative means of expressing it.

Openings can be one or more paragraphs, although for most compositions, particularly with novice writers, a one-paragraph opening is sufficient. Most essays feature a claim or thesis in the opening and then present the author's reasons or points, previewed in the order in which they will be developed in the body of the essay. Most openings also include one or more of the following:

1. Background or contextual information to help the reader relate the topic to the prompt or context. For example, an opening involving a specific work would include its title and author. A report on a historical or scientific event might establish dates relevant to the event.

2. One or two statements that tell the reader the purpose for the composition. For example, writers can state whether they are arguing a point or examining an issue.

3. A controlling idea (claim or thesis) that is knowledgeable, clear, and credible. Ask students to work in pairs to review and refine their temporary claims or theses.

4. A brief list of the main reasons or points they will present in the main body of the composition.

First sentence. An opening to a good composition starts with a sentence (or two) that creates the first connection between reader and writer. A weak opening sentence will not draw readers into the text. However, a strong, purposeful start will invite readers to engage. In formal writing, the starting sentences of the opening section do not aim to grab attention in the way they might in a news article, but they do attempt to get readers' attention by framing a problem or topic in some meaningful way and help readers gain some insight into the topic and purpose.

Below are strategies writers use to engage readers and establish a context for their expository texts. Note that during this stage, students also establish tone and voice, making decisions about whether language should be informal or formal, or somewhere in between, starting with the first sentence:

- **Restate the prompt** in your own words and provide an answer or position. This is a no-fail way to start, especially for the student who is new at writing essays or who tends to stray from the prompt and lose focus. A student writing about butterfly migratory paths might restate a prompt about butterfly migratory paths, "Butterflies, one of the natural world's most delicate creatures, weigh only milligrams and yet travel thousands of miles each year."
- **Start with a grand, sweeping generalization.** An example is this famous opening statement from Rousseau's *Social Contract*: "Man was born free, and he is everywhere in chains" (1762).
- **Start with a question.** A question can capture the reader's attention as well as provide a question to answer in a composition, as does Sojourner Truth in her famous speech "Ain't I a Woman?"
- **Start with an example.** Read and analyze professional works to gain insight into how authors use examples or anecdotes to help readers understand a problem or situation. Students should be able to find such examples in a range of articles, including science and general news articles.
- **Start with a "grounding" statement** in which the writer provides background and context for the argument or explanation, as did Abraham Lincoln in his Gettysburg Address: "Four score and seven years ago . . ." (1863).

Opening paragraph. Once a student's first sentence is on the page, it's time to build a fully developed opening paragraph or, for those who can manage it, an opening section. Encourage students to experiment with this paragraph by composing two or three different versions using the start-up strategies above. Here are examples of openings from student compositions in Appendix C of the Common Core State Standards:

Grade 4: *Dear Mr. _____ and Mrs. _____,*
We have a problem. The wildlife here in _____ is very limited. There is not a lot of opportunity to learn about conservation and wildlife preservation. If we took a field trip to _____, our problem would be solved. _____, _____, _____, and I would like to take our class for a great learning experience. In addition, we will provide a study guide to _____ to identify the animals and provide information about conservation of endangered wildlife. (National Governors Association Center for Best Practices & Council of Chief State School Officers, 2010a, p. 25)

Grade 7: *My report is on a very rare and unique wetland that many people do not even know exists. They occur only in a few places around the world. My topic is created by a specific geographical condition. Vernal pools in San Diego occur only on the local mesas and terraces, where soil conditions allow, but these are the ideal place for much of the city's urban and agricultural development. Is it possible to find a balance between the two conflicting purposes of expansion and preservation? This raises an interesting question; how can you establish vernal pools being thought of as a geographical asset?* (National Governors Association Center for Best Practices & Council of Chief State School Officers, 2010a, p. 42)

Grade 10: *In the novel* Animal Farm, *by George Orwell, there is one very particular character whose pride and selfishness creates problems. This character had just merely good ideas in the beginning. However, as time went on, his true self-interest began to shine through. This character started a free republic of animals and turned it into a plantation that used animals as slaves. He never did have enough and always wanted more, regardless of the price that others had to pay. This character whose pride and selfishness creates problems is none other than the great leader of Animal Farm himself, comrade Napolean [Napoleon], the pig.* (National Governors Association Center for Best Practices & Council of Chief State School Officers, 2010a, p. 68)

Reminder: Leave time for feedback. At this and for every stage in the DWC, provide opportunities to obtain feedback from another student, group of students, or you. Feedback doesn't have to be elaborate or even notes on paper. Giving guidance at the beginning of the writing process can help students stay on task and establish a sharp focus for the remaining composition. Consider having students work in pairs and read their own opening paragraphs aloud, taking notes on their own and each other's first drafts. Also try walking around your classroom, pointing out to students what is and isn't working while providing hints about how to improve the passages. It only takes a minute or two, but the payoff for your students is significant. If a student is confused about the assignment or hasn't fully responded, you can provide immediate feedback and motivation.

Writing an Initial Draft

Now that students have a first paragraph, they are ready to write the development section or body of the composition. Have students keep their outlines handy. The first draft is a multiparagraph composition in which students transform their notes and outlines into fully structured compositions for the first time. You taught them to plan ahead for this stage when you gave them strategies for shaping their ideas during the prewriting stages. Students who included sufficient detail in outlines can now focus on writing clear, coherent sentences because they have already made all the other relevant decisions about paragraphing.

The production of the first draft is often an untidy process, so don't expect a polished composition. But you should expect an emerging structure and sense of logic along with some reference to texts or sources. During this stage, students should return to the prompt and their text often to ensure they stay on task. You should always post the assignment prompt prominently so that you can point to it as you check in with students.

The basic structure for the development of a composition is, of course, body paragraphs, with each paragraph containing a topic sentence followed by evidence in some form—examples, data, quotes, or an author's statement or research findings. By the end of middle school, students should be learning techniques for elaborating on ideas and developing their logic. For example, they should be interlacing explanatory passages that link topic sentences (reasons or points) more closely to evidence as they address the charge in the assignment. In this development paragraph, a student writer provides a good example by elaborating on the meaning of John Donne's famous phrase:

> One of the articles we looked at was Meditation XVII by John Donne. He said, "No man is an island." This really moved me. It showed me that we are all in this together and none of us are alone. We are a whole continent and if something happens to part of it or a group of people it happens to all of us or the whole continent. So we need to help even if it did not happen to "our side."

Structural templates. Some students may need a template to help them develop a structure for their writing. Like an architect's blueprint, a template delineates the basic structure and guides construction. In one sense, the outline has already done this, establishing an organization and sequence of ideas for students' compositions. However, some students may need more support. Your template should help students manage the specific structural elements necessary to develop a line of thought.

A prototype template for an argumentative essay involves an opening paragraph, some number of body paragraphs each stating a reason and including evidence, and a closing paragraph. A template for an explanatory essay or informative report includes an opening paragraph, some number of paragraphs each with a relevant point to include examples or references, and a closing paragraph. When constructing a template, pay attention to the verbs. A cause-and-effect essay, for example, would require at least four paragraphs or sections: an opening, a section on "cause" and one on "effect," and one for closure.

Writing teachers often use templates (see the examples in Figures 5.2 and 5.3) to provide students with an organizer for the various structures for comparison, description, and other organizational patterns common to expository writing. These come in handy for all writers from time to time, but particularly for inexperienced writers and verbose writers who need boundaries. As you teach writing assignments, collect templates. As students gain more skill and independence as writers, they can choose to use them or not.

Figure 5.2

Student Writing Template for Argumentation

Title:

Author:

Date:

School and Subject/Class:

Opening: Address the prompt by starting with a question, quote, or background to the topic. Provide the reader with a context by providing background or situational details. Be sure to end by stating your claim. The opening can be one or two paragraphs.

Counterclaim: Address one or more counterclaims, and explain why they are weak or irrelevant in a "However . . ." statement.

Development: Develop your argument by laying out your reasons. Each paragraph contains a reason statement and provides evidence from texts, data, or other sources. You can have as many reasons as you need to make your case.

Reason 1: State your reason in a sentence or two. Provide evidence to explain or support your reason.

Reason 2: State your next reason in a sentence or two. Provide evidence to explain or support your reason.

Reason 3: Continue developing your logic with additional reasons as needed to strengthen your position.

Closure: Restate your claim in a new way, and sum up the reasons why you have taken this position. Draw a conclusion that relates to the prompt or the audience in some specific way.

Revising a Draft

During the first and subsequent drafts, you will find that conferences with individual students open up opportunities for teachable moments that might not occur in a whole-class lesson. These short but important encounters are best managed through coaching techniques since each student composes differently, even on the same assignment. Good writing coaches walk around the classroom to ensure students get the claim or thesis right and spend time conferencing in short sessions during the drafting and revision stages. A two-minute conversation can help a student refine a phrase or see a flaw in logic that, with your help, he can revise. It's a somewhat messy process because coaching causes students to reflect and

---

Figure 5.3

Student Writing Template for a Numerical Report

[OFFICE NAME] REPORT— Produced by [Office Section or Branch]

Publication Date: MM/DD/YYYY

Version: {EX. V1 or V4.11:55.AM}

Title of Report/Information Request:

Introduction: Provide a statement that summarizes the requested information; include relevant dates and the context for which the data are necessary.

Methodology: Describe how the results in the "Analysis" tab were derived, including what databases were used, what restrictions were used on the queries (date restrictions, variable restrictions, etc.), what dates were used (filing date, case created date, etc.), and what years (fiscal or calendar). Also specify any caveats to the data such as known data quality issues.

Results: Summarize the tables and graphs presented in the "Analysis" tab.

Discussion: Provide a short discussion or summary of the findings and their relevance. For example, are the results historically significant? Do they appear to be an aberration compared to what has been found previously?

Glossary: If there are terms that may be foreign or new, add any terms and definitions that are directly related to comprehending the data. The glossary is particularly helpful for clients external to our office.

change their minds, and you can see this messiness on their papers. This is in the nature of the drafting process, and with your guidance, students eventually find the clarity of thought they are looking for. Try not to edit for grammar or conventions at this stage. Instead, prompt students with questions or work with them to find the language they are searching for to clarify their thinking or point: "Tell me in a few sentences what you want to say." "Can you find a better word here that your audience would understand?" "Where is your controlling idea?" "Can you say more about this point or give an example?"

Now that students have written a first draft, they are ready to pay close attention to the development of their ideas, their use of evidence, and their clarity of expression. The first drafts should show some emerging traits you ultimately expect to see in their final compositions, but at this point key details or some aspects of the assignment are probably missing.

During the revision stage of the Writing Sequence is when you should focus your attention on refining the structure of your students' essays as well as their thinking.

Word processing programs are enormously helpful in making the revising and editing stages less tedious. In order to ensure students have enough text to work with, suggest that they add a certain amount of material to each paragraph in this first draft (e.g., a certain number of sentences or supporting details). Once the text is written out or keyed in, students will find the revision and editing stages much easier.

Because revising a full draft is demanding work, you may want to focus on only a few elements in each revision, such as the opening, types of evidence, or relevancy of evidence. Revising a composition may be the most important stage in the entire production process because it's the stage where students refine their thinking and their ability to organize that thinking clearly. If possible, students should make at least two revisions after the first draft, one focused on reasoning or logic and the other on relevancy or evidence. In both cases, they should examine the overall organization of the composition to make sure that it still reflects their thinking. If you have the time and your class is not too weary of the assignment, more revisions will help students continue to develop both thinking and fluency. Below are some ways to focus the revision process so that it doesn't seem too overwhelming:

- Identify a single trait (e.g., "Does each paragraph contain a topic sentence?") and ask students to check their drafts for this trait. You can repeat this with different traits. This is a good pair/share exercise.
- Have each student choose a problematic passage and read it aloud to a small group. The group's charge is to help the student clarify the passage.
- Use the rubric as a comment sheet. Identify only the areas that need work, with the expectation that students will improve these traits. Save time on scoring the final copies by having students score early drafts on specific traits and then revise those traits.

- Create an area in your classroom where students can gather to work on passages in their compositions together, using peer feedback to improve their work. All you need is a simple arrangement consisting of a document projector or a computer plus a table and chairs.

Note that each of these suggestions involves students working in pairs or in small groups to assist each other in analyzing and then revising their drafts. Discussion at this stage in the DWC is just as important as it is earlier in the process when your students discussed a text in order to generate understanding. At this stage, however, the goal is not understanding as much as it is clarity and coherence. All writers need readers at this stage to help them "see" the text with fresh eyes, and these variations on group work are designed to give each student writer the most pertinent and helpful feedback.

It is important that every time your students sit together during the revision and editing processes they have clear instructions and goals, as well as clear roles to play at each point in the process. During revision, in particular, it is important that individual students read their early drafts aloud to other students while those students take notes on their responses. While reading aloud, the original authors will hear and "see" passages they want to repair or clarify even before they receive feedback from the others in the group. In this way, they get a double dose of formative assessment: self-assessment as well as feedback from the other group members. Finally, when one writer hears or sees a particularly effective passage in another student's essay, she can also learn a strategy through osmosis.

Editing and Publishing

Editing is the stage that offers you opportunities for teaching the importance of writing conventions as a means to communicating with clarity. Now that students have revised their draft compositions for structure and coherence, they are ready to receive feedback on the details of grammar, spelling, and punctuation. Activities for helping students both peer- and self-edit include the following:

- **Copyediting.** Post spelling, grammar items, or conventions that you must see correctly written in their papers, such as transition words or quotation marks. Teach students publisher's editing marks.
- **Error analysis.** Signal where errors occur by placing a check at the end of a line, using one check for each error. Students must find the errors on their own. If students are stuck after three tries, they can ask you for more direction. You can have students create a graph showing how many errors they have per number of words, with the goal of reducing this ratio over time. Have students use error analysis on each other's drafts.
- **Prose analysis.** A teacher of business and technical writing devised this method. Direct students to circle any forms of the "to be" verb—*is, are, was, were,* and so on. Use this exercise to teach the difference between active and passive voice and when to use each. The teacher developed this method to help engineers eliminate the overuse of passive sentences in their reports, which obscured the agent in these sentences. Use this method with prepositions and other overused language terms, such as *they* and *it.* Once these items are identified, have students rewrite sentences for better clarity (Lanham, 2006).
- **Word processing.** Teach students to use computer tools to edit their work, paying attention to the green and red markings that appear. More resources using technology are coming into the market to support instruction at this stage, so consider these for your classroom.
- **Identifying long or awkward sentences.** Have each author identify the five longest sentences in her composition and then work with a partner to ensure that each sentence is clear on a first reading. This may involve cutting excess words or dividing a long sentence into two shorter, clearer sentences.
- **Identifying sentence fragments.** Have students work in pairs to identify any sentence fragments in both their compositions.

Then have the original authors add the necessary elements to create complete sentences.

Here again, make sure students use the speaking and listening skills they practiced during the Discourse Sequence to help each other edit the final drafts of their papers by asking each other clarifying questions. The more of this work they can do together in pairs or small groups with clear roles and goals, the more they will collectively learn from the process and the better the individual writing will become.

Students now have a copy of their work almost ready for publication. Be sure to help them see how their final copies should be readable and neat and in the format appropriate to the protocols of a discipline. This is the stage to insert graphics or illustrations. Give students specific guidelines and point out this is what journals and professors require. These might include the following:

- Titling, spacing, and font specifications
- Name, date, and course
- An abstract or summary
- Proper citations for source material
- Graphics, illustrations, or tables
- A bibliography

If you have identified an authentic audience for your writing assignment, students are now in a position to receive real-world feedback from that audience. One reason we stress the term *publication* in relation to the final draft is that a real audience motivates students and provides a reason to celebrate at the end of the process. In addition, certain audiences can also provide the students with authentic feedback that is at least as valuable as that provided by a teacher.

Celebrate!

You and your students have managed a complex task, and you should celebrate this occasion in some way. Some teachers focus on rewarding the students for their persistence and effort. Teachers often find a way to make their students' works public in order to show students that their written work has relevance outside of the classroom. Some have had students publish a journal either online or in print; some have published print anthologies of student work for circulation through the local library and school media center. Some have invited professionals to discuss the assignment's topic with students. A high school teacher we know invited an elected official to participate in a seminar on the role of government with her students after they had read several historic works and written on the topic.

* * *

The DWC is intended to help you teach your students how to think and communicate with precision and clarity. We know that this approach to teaching speaking, listening, and writing may seem like a long, involved endeavor, but the time and effort will pay off as students acquire more speed and facility. Their improved discussion skills will generate more ideas to use in their writing, and consistent practice with the writing process will help them express those ideas clearly and coherently.

💡 CHECK YOUR THINKING

Ms. Chavez, a high school teacher, sees 185 students a day in her history classes. Despite having so many students and therefore so many papers to read, she is determined to engage students in discourse and writing assignments. What might you suggest to Ms. Chavez to make her work manageable?

See Appendix C (p. 162) for possible responses.

6

Putting Discourse, Writing, and Thinking into Action

Reading maketh a full man; conference a ready man; and writing an exact man.

—Francis Bacon, *The Philosophical Works of Francis Bacon*

What does the Discourse and Writing Cycle look like when fully implemented with experienced students? What is the full measure of the literacy process like for both teacher and students? This chapter offers an example of the fully realized DWC in an 8th grade science class, where the teacher is dedicated to training his students to think critically through formal discussion and writing. Although this is a middle school class, the process is the same for all grades, 4–12.

Maynard is an 8th grade science teacher at a large, urban middle school in the Midwest. As part of an innovative effort to implement the Common Core State Standards in conjunction with 21st century skills, he assigns four full literacy units during the year. This is the second year in which Maynard and his colleagues have had their students read seminal works in scientific thought, discuss these works in a series of Paideia seminars, and write about them extensively. In addition to the series of classroom-based reading, discussion, and writing, students also read contemporary scientific articles of their own choosing (from a list prepared by Maynard and his colleagues) and keep a course journal in which they write about their personal reading. This last strategy is designed to teach independent reading and writing habits that complement the more formal work done in class. The students also develop a personal glossary, in which they describe in detail a minimum of five new words encountered each week (pronunciation, etymology, definitions, sample usage, etc.) from their ongoing reading, discussion, and writing.

During the second semester, Maynard and his students read and discuss in detail an excerpt from Copernicus's *The Revolutions of the Heavenly Spheres* as part of an extended literacy unit structured in part by the following writing task:

> *Why do some scientific discoveries cause so much controversy? After reading and discussing an excerpt from Copernicus's* The Revolutions of the Heavenly Spheres, *write a fully developed essay that explains why Copernicus's ideas were so controversial when they first appeared. Be sure to support your position with evidence from the text.*

Maynard knew full well how demanding the task he had set his students with this assignment was. He discussed with them in detail how a successful reply to the writing prompt required a clear understanding of several things: (1) What was the prevailing view of the universe prior to Copernicus, (2) how did Copernicus's discoveries alter this view, and (3) why was this shift in understanding so threatening to so many people? To help students build the necessary background information, he provided them with a set of articles for independent reading that filled in the historical context. The students could cite these articles in their essays.

As a final element in this introductory discussion of the assignment, the students asked how they would be assessed. Maynard was pleased because he had taught his students never to begin the seminar and writing process without knowing who their audience was and how their work would be evaluated. He told them, "Your audience is other middle school science teachers and students from across the country. This is the third of our four essays from this year, and we will collect and publish these last two essays on our class website. Your grade will be a combination of self-assessment, writing group peer assessment, and my assessment of your work at each stage in the process."

"That's too much work. Why don't you just grade the final paper?"

"Yeah," another student joined in. "You can't expect us to both write the essay and grade it too!"

Maynard responded, "You and the other students in your writing group know more about how hard you've worked on this assignment than I do. And if I work with you to assess your work all the way through the various stages in the process, then the final papers should be all but perfect. Remember, our goal is to produce 26 essays worthy of being published on the class website—26 papers we can all be proud of."

What Maynard didn't say, because the students already knew it, is that he would read each student's paper twice—once quickly at the revision stage, when he would give broad feedback toward the next draft, and again once they were finalized, when he would discuss them in a series of individual writing conferences. The students also knew that as their "editor," he would help them all he could but, ultimately, the quality of the published work was up to them.

Just before the students filed out of class at the end of this first period in the scientific revolutions unit, Maynard asked, as he often did: "What's our motto?" The students chanted in response just as they'd been trained: "Scientists investigate! Scientists discuss! Scientists write!"

READING AND DISCUSSING COPERNICUS: THE DISCOURSE SEQUENCE

The class spent three days on the Discourse Sequence, the first sequence in the DWC. On the first day, they did an inspectional read of the excerpt from *The Revolutions of the Heavenly Spheres* by skimming through it and discussing the format. The students added words like *infinite, sphere,* and *superfluous* to their glossaries during this first exposure to the text. Maynard then read the entire excerpt aloud slowly, while students highlighted more unfamiliar words. He then read the text again, sentence by sentence, while the entire class discussed the difficult vocabulary. He explained that they were going to do their Paideia seminar two days later, after the class had a chance to do some background reading on Copernicus and his theory that earth and the other planets orbited around the sun.

On the day prior to the seminar, Maynard divided the class into six reading groups and handed out three different articles on the theories of the universe and earth's place in it. The articles dealt with the shock waves that resulted from the work of scientists like Galileo and Copernicus. Groups A and B read the first article and took notes; Groups C and D, the second article; and Groups E and F, the third article. Once the student groups had a chance to read and discuss their articles, Maynard had them switch into discussion groups, where each student summarized his or her article for students from the other groups. For the last 10 minutes of the period, he led the entire class in a summary discussion of what they had learned, gleaning the following background information with the students' help:

- Copernicus was one of several mathematician-scientists who developed the theory of a sun-centered universe.
- Prior to Copernicus (and the others), people commonly thought that the sun and other heavenly bodies orbited around the earth.
- The Catholic Church led the attacks on Copernicus and the other scientists, claiming that they were promoting heretical ideas.
- Copernicus based his theory on his observations of the heavenly bodies, using telescopes developed by other scientists.
- Math played a role in Copernicus's theory (but the students weren't sure how).

Maynard posted these five insights on the whiteboard in class, and the students added the articles to their unit folders.

On the day of the seminar, just prior to the discourse, Maynard had his students read the Copernicus excerpt for a third time. This time, he assigned each of the 20 sentences in the text to a student and had them paraphrase the sentences in modern English. He circulated while they worked, helping those students who had drawn the longest, most difficult sentences. The class then worked through the text one last time, sharing their paraphrases out loud.

During the seminar itself, the students were seated in a circle so that they could communicate directly with each other. They analyzed both the surface meaning of the text and the implications of the ideas being put forth by Copernicus. Near the end of the seminar, Maynard asked them to reflect on how this view of the universe was different from the one that preceded it. The resulting discourse ranged far and wide, covering a number of perspectives. For his closing question, he then asked the students: "How does it make you feel to know that your home—the earth—is one of a number of planets orbiting the sun rather than the main planet in the center of the universe?" The students offered a number of insights about how their sense of importance was related to their "position" in the universe.

CONSIDERING COPERNICUS: THE TRANSITION TO WRITING SEQUENCE

Immediately following the seminar and process debriefing, Maynard posted the initial question from the writing prompt on his whiteboard:

Why do some scientific discoveries cause so much controversy?

He then instructed his students to write for 10 minutes without stopping, jotting down everything they remembered saying or hearing during the seminar that was related to this question. They were not to worry about punctuation or grammar, "just grab the ideas while they're fresh." This exercise—Capturing the Discussion—is the first stage in the Transition to Writing Sequence, and Maynard wanted his students to record what they had heard, said, and thought while their memories of the discussion were fresh. He then told the students to come to class the next day with everything they needed to continue the Transition to Writing Sequence of the cycle.

The next day in class, Maynard took his students directly into identifying potential evidence for their essays. He first displayed the writing task and led the class through a recap of their original analysis of the assignment. He then outlined their work for the rest of the period. First, they would draft their thesis statements and share a copy with him in writing. Second, they would use their draft thesis statements as well as their post-seminar notes from the day before as a starting point in choosing the two or more reasons why scientific discoveries, such as Copernicus's theory, are often so controversial. Once they identified the two or more reasons they wanted to explore, they would then begin combing through the text selecting specific passages to either quote or cite. To help them do this, Maynard handed out a simple, full-page graphic organizer like the one in Figure 6.1.

Figure 6.1

Copernicus Graphic Organizer

Some scientific discoveries are so controversial because _____
_____ .

Copernicus's Theory	Reason #1	Reason #2	Reason #3
Passages to quote			
Passages to cite			

Halfway through the period, he took up his copies of the student thesis statements, promising a quick read and response the following day. Maynard then set his students to work searching for textual evidence to explicate or support their arguments.

At the beginning of class the next day, he returned the students' definitions, each with a handwritten note along with edits designed to help his students produce clear, coherent cause-and-effect statements.

They devoted the rest of the period to the second stage of the Transition to Writing Sequence, Structuring the Writing. Because his students were relatively experienced writers at this point in their middle school careers, Maynard didn't give them a template for the essay but, rather, questioned them about how they might organize and present their arguments. Over the next 45 minutes, the students came up with several acceptable patterns or designs for the essay. By the end of the period, his whiteboard showed two versions of a possible design, as shown in Figure 6.2.

Figure 6.2	
Blueprints for an Essay on Copernicus	
Design 1	**Design 2**
Introduction: Scientific discoveries that were revolutionary; reasons why Main Body 1: The universe before Copernicus Main Body 2: What Copernicus said Main Body 3: The universe after Copernicus; why the change was so radical Conclusion: Other scientific discoveries that changed our view of the universe	Introduction: Why some scientific discoveries are so controversial; two reasons why Copernicus is an example of this Main Body 1: First reason why Main Body 2: Second reason why Main Body 3: Before and after Copernicus Conclusion: Copernicus as an example of reason 1 and reason 2

Just before the end of this design period, one of Maynard's better writing students raised her hand and asked, "What if we combine elements from the two designs? I like the introduction and conclusion from the first design, but I also want to begin and end my paper with Copernicus. I want to mix and match."

Maynard replied, "I like the way you're thinking. The designs on the board are only suggestions for structuring your compositions. Either of these will work as long as you make your structure explicit. And of course, you can mix features from both. Just be sure you know why you're choosing the pattern that you end up with."

The homework assignment for that night was for each student to craft a structure for the essay and decide which reasons to use at what points in the paper. Maynard was especially pleased when one of his quietest students visited him before homeroom the next morning with an entirely different design that he had worked out with his older sister's help. It was more sophisticated than the two that were still displayed on the board, but it made perfect sense with his ideas, so Maynard encouraged him to use it, promising to help if the student got stuck during the Writing Sequence.

WRITING ABOUT COPERNICUS: THE WRITING SEQUENCE

That day, during class, the students focused on the first stage in the Writing Sequence, Crafting an Opening. Maynard reminded his students that their introductory paragraphs should clearly state a cause-and-effect thesis and preview the main bodies of their papers. Several of the students decided to split the introductory elements into two paragraphs: one that focused on scientific discoveries in general and one on Copernicus in particular. Maynard encouraged them to try this tactic, noting that they'd always have a chance to revise. While the students worked, he circulated through the room, coaching and encouraging, constantly murmuring his mantra about introductions: "Clarity, clarity, clarity. In order to be interesting, you first have to be clear."

The next day, students spent the entire class period composing the first draft of the complete essay. They used their copies of the text as well as the background articles, their notes on the seminar, and their detailed outlines. During this period, Maynard tried to stay figuratively out of their way while they worked, only visiting students at their desks when a hand in the air or a pleading look gained his attention. He noticed that many of his students were struggling with how to quote the text in their papers, whether they were using short passages or long, and he made a mental note to give a brief lecture before the revision stage, using examples to show them how to insert the quotes. By the end of the period, the majority of students had all or most of their first drafts finished, and he called a halt to the writing 10 minutes before the bell. "In writing about Copernicus, what have you learned?" he asked.

"About science or about myself?" one student asked.

"Both," he replied.

"I've learned that science affects how we view ourselves. Even when we don't realize it, we mostly take on the currently accepted scientific view of things."

"What else? What happens when that view changes?" Maynard asked.

"Then we have to change as well," another student added. "Change or get left behind."

The next day in class, Maynard led the students through the first of two revisions that they would do during the revision stage. The first was for thinking, and the second, for structure. He gave a short didactic lesson on how to quote and cite the text, putting examples of both short, embedded quotes and longer, indented quotes on the board. Then he led his students through the first round of revision by dividing them up into groups of three and giving them the following instructions:

> We will do two rounds of revision on this paper because it should represent both our best thinking and our best writing. During the first round, we will address the clarity and cohesion of our thinking. I have divided you into groups of three so that every writer will have the benefit of two critical but friendly perspectives. I want you to take turns reading your papers aloud and receiving warm and cool feedback on how clearly you develop your argument. While writer A reads his or her paper, I expect B and C to take notes on the clarity of the following items [here he referred his students to the board]:
>
> - The cause-and-effect thesis statement
> - The topic sentences of the various paragraphs
> - The relationship of the topic sentences to the thesis statement
>
> Once writer A has finished reading, I would like B and C to offer "warm" and "cool" feedback by saying, "I really like the way you ..." (warm) and "I wonder if you've thought about ..." (cool), while writer A takes detailed notes. And then I want you to repeat the cycle with the other two

writers. And by now, you know me well enough to know that I expect you to take this process very seriously, as it is the key to producing a collection of thoughtful, coherent papers.

During the revision group work, Maynard circulated through the room, listening closely to the various groups and taking notes without interrupting the students. When all the groups were finished, he explained that they would repeat the process one more time on the following day. In the meantime, the students should revise their papers in response to the suggestions they'd received from their two partners. He also explained that at the end of the following class period he would take up the revised drafts so that he could add his comments on the clarity of his students' thinking.

The next day, the same groups repeated the process, but this time, the two listeners were assigned the following task:

Yesterday, we focused on thinking, and today we're going to focus on writing. While you are reading your essay today, I want you to actually slow down and read more slowly, pausing at the end of each sentence. While writer A is reading, I want B and C to note at least two sentences you think are particularly effective and two sentences that confuse or mislead you. When A has finished reading, both B and C need to identify which sentences they particularly like and which two are confusing while writer A takes notes. And then repeat the cycle with the other two papers.

Once again, Maynard circulated, taking notes of his own. This time, he paid particular attention to the groups that didn't seem to be working as well together and in a few instances, coached the process itself rather than the content. After the students had taken a few minutes to revise those sentences that their partners found confusing, Maynard took up their drafts to read over the weekend—emphasizing that they would be returned with comments.

On the following Monday, he gave the papers back at the beginning of the period, and the students spent the time producing one more draft for the next day's editing session. Again Maynard circulated, explaining his own comments in a few instances and showing students how to clarify certain passages that their readers found confusing. In a few cases, he encouraged students to add more detail, including more direct references to the text or articles to support their theses. On the following day, he divided the students into groups of three one last time, this time for surface editing. He had them emphasize two elements that he had noticed when reading their drafts: run-on sentences and insertion of quotes. He first gave a short mini-lesson on each before assigning students to their groups and giving them the following directions:

> I have divided you up into your same groups of three again, but this time, the protocol will be different. This time, we're going to read each other's papers slowly and silently. During the next 30 minutes, I want you to read each of your partners' papers slowly and mark any comma error you find and any problem with the use of quoted material. If you see something else you think might be a problem, like a misspelled word, underline it and put a small question mark beside it; it will be up to the original writer to correct. While you are working, I will circulate. If you aren't sure about a run-on sentence or quotation issue, raise your hand, and we will consult. Our goal is for there to be NO—and I repeat, NO—errors of this sort in our final drafts.

Maynard consulted frequently during the following 30 minutes, most often by deferring the question to the group of three students and leading them to the right editorial conclusion by asking questions rather than fixing the problem himself. In each case, though, he didn't leave a group until the issue was resolved correctly.

With this final editing stage completed, Maynard negotiated a deadline for the final papers to be submitted for compilation and editing. During the follow-up days before the final draft was due, he gave his students time to catch up on other classwork, particularly their vocabulary glossaries, while he facilitated a series of brief (average time five minutes) assessment conferences, to which students brought the following artifacts from previous work:

- Their marked-up versions of the text (Discourse Sequence)
- Their self-assessment documents from the seminar process (Discourse Sequence)
- Their original Transition to Writing notes (Transition to Writing Sequence)
- Their definitions and thesis statements (Transition to Writing Sequence)

- Their essay designs (Transition to Writing Sequence)
- Their multiple drafts (Writing Sequence)

During the conferences, he had the students self-assess three things: their participation in their revision and editing groups, the extent to which their essays had improved during revision and editing, and the extent to which they had achieved the vision represented in their designs. While they filled out a simple self-assessment form, he assigned a score to their artifacts, referring to his notes as needed. At the end of the conference, he and the individual student compared notes and totaled the points from both sets of scores, so that the only missing ingredient to a final grade would be his reading of the final draft. Because he had trained them well during the course of the year, and coached the DWC assiduously, his students were almost all going to score an *A* or *B* for the process leading up to the final draft. As he kept repeating, he expected all of the essays to be *A* papers by the time they were ready to be uploaded to the class website.

There is one final note about the DWC as practiced by this teacher: When Maynard first started using an extended literacy process two years before, all of his student papers had been handwritten, even in multiple drafts. Once he had access to a computer lab in his school, so that all of his students were able to use a word processing program to produce multiple drafts, he switched to that medium to make his students' lives easier and their products easier to read—but only when *all* students had equal access to computers. "In my opinion, the Writing Sequence has never been about word processing tricks and spell-check programs. In fact, in some ways, word processing makes the revision and editing process so much quicker and easier that students forget to take the time to think about what they're saying. And I find myself telling them more and more to *slow down* . . . so they have time to think about what they're writing. Anytime the thought process is involved, both conversation and writing take time." When asked if he's ever had problems with plagiarism, he laughs. "If my students do what I ask, then we have walked together through each and every step of the process, and it is all but impossible for them to plagiarize. Or if they accidentally do borrow from another source, then both their classmates and I are standing by watching, and we catch it. Is it impossible for them to borrow? Of course not. But they know full well that they've betrayed their writing teammates if they use other material without citation and betrayed their own interests in preparing for high school and college."

When Maynard asked his students what title and epigraph they wanted him to use in the website file containing their essays, they asked what an *epigraph* was. He told them that it was the pithy quote at the front of a book that set the stage for what was to follow. He knew he didn't need to remind them to add the word to their glossaries. After some lively discussion, the students asked that he title the collection of online essays *Scientific Revolution!* For an epigraph, they settled on the working motto that he had taught them from the first day of class: "Scientists investigate! Scientists discuss! Scientists write!"

CHECK YOUR THINKING

How does Maynard's full use of the Discourse and Writing Cycle encourage students to think about the science curriculum at a deeper level?

See Appendix C (p. 162) for possible responses.

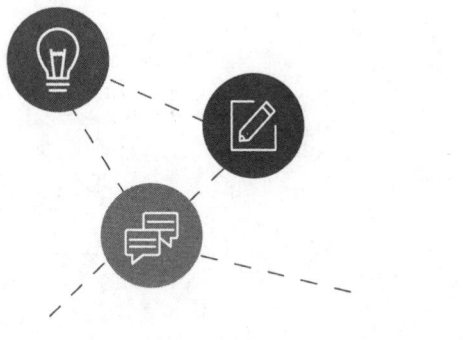

PART

3

The Discourse and Writing Cycle in the Disciplines

In Part 3, we discuss in detail how to develop the Discourse and Writing Cycle in English language arts (Chapter 7), history or social studies (Chapter 8), and science and math classrooms (Chapter 9). In Chapter 10, we provide detailed DWC lesson plans for elementary, middle, and high school for a variety of subjects.

7

DWC in the English Classroom

Beauty is harder to analyze than truth.

—Mortimer J. Adler and Charles van Doren, *How to Read a Book*

Seminar discourse and writing in the English language arts class is, in some ways, a challenge because it has traditionally been assumed that language arts is not just the most natural place for discussion and writing instruction—it's the *only* place. This incorrect assumption placed all the pressure for teaching speaking, listening, and writing skills squarely on the shoulders of language arts teachers, many of whom were trained to teach literature, not formal discussion and writing. As high-stakes, standardized testing has played a larger and larger role in the profession during recent years, many language arts teachers have quite naturally bowed to the pressure to only teach the kind of writing that was being tested—relatively short, unimaginative pieces produced in one draft under tremendous time pressure. What we have described here as the Discourse and Writing Cycle has become increasingly rare in the elementary and middle school language arts classroom, in part because of time pressure and in part because the process itself wasn't "tested."

The good news is that national and international forces such as the 21st century skills inventories and the Common Core State Standards are freeing language arts teachers to once again teach speaking, listening, and writing skills as they should be taught—as exploration and reflection of the curriculum, not as just another testable skill. These forces also mean that coming years should see more professional development opportunities for language arts teachers to practice their own discussion and writing skills while teaching their students how to discuss, write, and think with rigor. In this chapter, we will focus on applying the DWC in a language arts classroom. In doing so, we never assume that the English teachers are the only ones teaching literacy but, rather, that they are the only ones teaching discussing and writing about literature as a way of understanding the world.

Two other key points are worth reiterating. First, college and career readiness implies an increased focus on teaching expository (rather than just narrative) writing in middle school and high school. Second, students should study the essay in its various forms as a model form of expository writing just as they study the other traditional genres (the novel, short story, poetry). The close study of especially well-made essays provides your students not only with thematic content to discuss but also with models for their own writing.

WHAT IDEAS ARE WORTH TALKING AND WRITING ABOUT?

During the 1950s, when Encyclopaedia Britannica was designing *Great Books of the Western World* (1952), Mortimer Adler and the editorial staff compiled a list of 102 Great Ideas that they "discovered" while indexing the collection. The Great Ideas in Figure 7.1 are listed in the end papers and discussed in detail in Volumes 2 and 3 of *Great Books*. This list of concepts, though in no way exhaustive, provides a handy starting place for thinking about the concepts that undergird most any curriculum at any grade.

One mistaken notion about the study of literature is that while it can be about anything, it is not by definition concerned with any one thing. A quick glance at the list quickly dispels this notion. Consider, for example, the following concepts: *art, definition, knowledge, language, memory and*

Figure 7.1		
Great Ideas		
ANGEL	HONOR	POETRY
ANIMAL	HYPOTHESIS	PRINCIPLE
ARISTOCRACY	IDEA	PROGRESS
ART	IMMORTALITY	PROPHECY
ASTRONOMY	INDUCTION	PRUDENCE
BEAUTY	INFINITY	PUNISHMENT
BEING	JUDGMENT	QUALITY
CAUSE	JUSTICE	QUANTITY
CHANCE	KNOWLEDGE	REASONING
CHANGE	LABOR	RELATION
CITIZEN	LANGUAGE	RELIGION
CONSTITUTION	LAW	REVOLUTION
COURAGE	LIBERTY	RHETORIC
CUSTOM AND CONVENTION	LIFE AND DEATH	SAME AND OTHER
DEFINITION	LOGIC	SCIENCE
DEMOCRACY	LOVE	SENSE
DESIRE	MAN	SIGN AND SYMBOL
DIALECTIC	MATHEMATICS	SIN
DUTY	MATTER	SLAVERY
EDUCATION	MECHANICS	SOUL
ELEMENT	MEDICINE	SPACE
EMOTION	MEMORY AND IMAGINATION	STATE
ETERNITY	METAPHYSICS	TEMPERANCE
EVOLUTION	MIND	THEOLOGY
EXPERIENCE	MONARCHY	TIME
FAMILY	NATURE	TRUTH
FATE	NECESSITY AND CONTIN-GENCY	TYRANNY
FORM		UNIVERSAL AND PARTICULAR
GOD	OLIGARCHY	VIRTUE AND VICE
GOOD AND EVIL	ONE AND MANY	WAR AND PEACE
GOVERNMENT	OPINION	WEALTH
HABIT	OPPOSITION	WILL
HAPPINESS	PHILOSOPHY	WISDOM
HISTORY	PHYSICS	WORLD
	PLEASURE AND PAIN	

Adapted from Adler, 1952.

imagination, poetry, rhetoric, sign and symbol, and *story.* In addition to these fundamental concepts that directly relate to literature and its role in our lives, there are also a number of secondary ideas that have to do with literature and how human beings use it to define themselves. Consider the following essential issues:

- The question of *truth,* as in fiction versus nonfiction
- The relationship of words and music, as in poetry
- The social function of words in political speeches and sermons
- The use of words in ritual performance, as in drama, religious services, and public celebration

All of these concepts can be explored, defined, and manipulated by students of literature in order to understand how they shape our lives.

This focus on units of study that address ideas fundamental to literature leads in turn to what is generally called genre study: a unit devoted to poetry, one to the short story, and so on. This design makes perfect sense so long as the teacher and students together address the *concept* of poetry and its role in society, not just read a series of poems and memorize poetic forms.

Another way of proceeding in course design, however, is to address any number of fundamental human concerns with literature as the medium. The list of possible ideas for a thematic study is all but endless, but consider these Great Ideas (again from Adler, 1952): *emotion, fate, good and evil, happiness, life and death, man* (i.e., *humankind), mind, power,* and *war and peace.*

What classifies writing as great "literature" is the richness and depth of the ideas the writer explores as well as his or her technique. The classics are a great place to begin in choosing a seminar text. From Cicero to Sandra Cisneros, "classic" works of literature are by definition packed with ideas and concepts.

The beauty of any unit of study driven by ideas is that it allows students to address a fundamental mystery and so gives their seminar discussion and writing a sense of authenticity and urgency that it could never have otherwise.

WHAT VOCABULARY IS WORTH TEACHING?

Just as it is generally—and mistakenly—assumed that it's the language arts teacher's job alone to teach literacy, it's also assumed that it's his job to teach vocabulary. This assumption often results in language arts teachers working their way through a predicated list with their students. This practice isn't necessarily a bad thing (unless it's only done as an isolated, mechanical exercise), but it's far from the only place in school in general or the language arts class in particular where vocabulary should be taught. Indeed, as David Liben of Student Achievement Partners pointed out to us in a recent conversation, vocabulary is the "acquisition of a domain" that requires constant development and exercise, never just manipulating a list of terms. In language arts class, there are at least three types of vocabulary that should be taught.

1. The first is the **vocabulary of standard usage** that allows students to understand, discuss, and edit their own writing. The eight parts of speech are a primary example from this glossary: *noun, verb, pronoun, adjective, adverb, conjunction, preposition,* and *interjection*. These terms are not the sole responsibility of the language arts teacher because students should be writing—and talking about their writing—in every subject area, but they are a primary, rather than secondary, concern in language arts.

2. The second kind of vocabulary is loosely called **literary terms:** words (and ideas) like *plot, setting, character,* and *theme.* A valuable resource of this kind of vocabulary is *A Handbook to Literature,* itself a modern classic and indispensable for any language arts teacher (most editions are credited to Thrall, Hibbard, and Holman, most recently edited by William Harmon [2012]). This handbook covers more than 2,000 literary terms and gives both teachers and students the tools they need to think and write about literature with increasing sophistication. Note that in addition to studying these two specific types of vocabulary native to English, students should also be learning how to decode unfamiliar words using context clues

and paying special attention to high-frequency words that they will encounter often in college and adult reading.

3. The third type of vocabulary is **high-frequency words**. These are the words that are of particular value because they open up a wide variety of reading experiences to students who are familiar with them. It is important to highlight high-frequency words because research clearly points to the value of exposing students to at least 30 new words per week, which in turn accelerates their reading ability as well as improving their speaking and writing.

WHAT TEXTS ARE WORTH TALKING AND WRITING ABOUT?

By definition the classics contain timeless ideas and values at any grade. The Greek myth "Cupid and Psyche" is a powerful text not just because it's an artifact from antiquity but because the narrative deals with *choice, power,* and *relationships.* Similarly, modern poet Richard Blanco's "One Today" is worthy of consideration not only because of vivid imagery but also because the poem addresses *identity, destiny,* and *choice.* In choosing literature worth seminar discussion and extended writing, the collection of ideas and values is paramount. The richer the set of ideas, the more one can find to think, talk, and write about.

In addition to richness in ideas and values, the appropriate degree of challenge is a primary consideration for text selection. You should choose literary texts that are just above your students' general reading level. Text difficulty is often based on vocabulary, which supports the practice of coaching students through vocabulary practice and multiple, focused readings. If you scaffold multiple readings of a challenging text with your students, you will automatically help them think critically about the ideas involved, preparing them to participate fully in seminar discussion and leading them in turn to produce more coherent, more sophisticated writing.

A final consideration when deciding on pieces of literature to include in a course is degree of relevance. Although teachers often make curriculum choices based on student interest, it's also important to talk about relevance through the ideas and values. Adolescents faced with *Romeo and Juliet*, for example, may not immediately relate to a play set hundreds of years ago in an Italian city-state. However, once they realize that the play is about the mysteries of sex, violence, and family conflict, they respond to the universal human relevance of the drama. Keeping the ideas and values front and center as a touchstone throughout the reading, discourse, and writing processes is a way to help students generate the energy necessary for understanding a complex text.

Consider a middle school language arts teacher in a rural western community who builds his syllabus out of series of rigorous literacy units, each of which is dedicated to an in-depth examination of a literary genre. This teacher, Paul, opens the year with his 6th grade literature students by assigning an "explanatory-definition" essay using James Hurst's short story "The Scarlet Ibis." Paul first reviews the standard definition of the short story as a literary form from *A Handbook to Literature* and then leads a Paideia seminar on the story. The text for this seminar is "The Scarlet Ibis," but he also displays the standard definition of the short story on the board, and his seminar questions are designed to help students consider if and how "The Scarlet Ibis" fulfills the characteristics of the definition.

Using a template task developed by the Literacy Design Collaborative (LDC), Paul wrote the following prompt to shape instruction throughout the unit:

> *What are the primary characteristics of the standard short story? After reading "The Scarlet Ibis" by James Hurst, write a literary review that defines the short story and explains how "The Scarlet Ibis" exemplifies this definition by describing at least three elements in the definition that are present in the story. Support your discussion with examples from the text.*

Paul's prompt sets up opportunities to teach a wide variety of literary vocabulary and assess his students' mastery of standard usage, so he will know what grammar and punctuation skills to teach in between this unit and the next. When he responds to the final drafts of his student essays, he does so with focused comments but no grade. He requires his students to reply to his comments with written notes about how they will improve their second essays in the course.

The second unit in Paul's "magical, mystery tour" (so named by the students) goes from the short story to the novel, so that students can focus on the differences (other than length) between the two forms. Normally, Paul teaches *To Kill a Mockingbird*, but this particular year, he has decided to use John Knowles's *A Separate Peace* so that he can work through the similarities between that novel and "The Scarlet Ibis" with his students. He coaches his students' reading of the novel by facilitating two formal seminars: one on the first chapter (before the students have read the rest of the novel) and one on the last. His writing assignment for this second unit of study raises the level of complexity. He uses another LDC Template Task to design a prompt that asks his students to compare the novel and the short story as fictional forms:

> *How is the novel different from the short story (other than length)? After reading* A Separate Peace *and "The Scarlet Ibis," write a young adult literary journal article in which you compare the novel and the short story. Support your discussion with evidence from the texts.*

Between the two assignments, Paul has stressed paragraph structure with his students, and in this second essay, he gives them several structural templates to choose from, but stresses essay structure and development during the revision and editing stages in the DWC.

During his unit on drama, Paul has his students read and discuss *Romeo and Juliet*. This choice leads to one especially dramatic Paideia seminar on the role of gender in human society, especially the differences between male and female characters—both in the play and in student experience. He then has students read a short story titled "A Jury of Her Peers" by Susan Glaspell and work in teams to write a reader's theater version of the play, translating it from prose to dramatic discourse. The students work their way through all the steps of the Writing Sequence, in this case focusing on producing the best possible dramatization of the story for presentation to other students and faculty.

During the poetry unit, Paul's students accuse him of being in love with Emily Dickinson. The students are intrigued by his description of her life and continue to laugh at his passion for her work. The seminar for this unit takes as its text two poems by Dickinson, and the seminar questions are focused on comparing the two works in terms of diction and imagery. In the writing task for this unit, Paul asks students to compare two poems written by the same poet from a list of paired poems that they have discussed in class—and argue that one is superior to the other. He explains that this is an argumentative comparison that asks them to first analyze each poem and then compare the two according to the complexity of the ideas and the ambiguity of the presentation. During this unit, the students read a wide variety of poets from around the world. For their essays they are allowed to choose any poet they want to consider.

The last unit in his course focuses on the personal essay as a literary genre. Paul believes that the one serious gap in most middle school language arts curricula is the lack of attention to nonfiction in general and to the personal essay in particular as a model for student writing. In this unit, he has students read and discuss a variety of essays and excerpts from longer, nonfiction works. The unit includes Paideia seminars on excerpts from nonfiction works having to do with the human relationship to non-human nature: short excerpts from Henry David Thoreau's *Walden* and Annie Dillard's *Pilgrim at Tinker Creek*. In the writing task for this unit, Paul asks his students to compare the two texts as essays, including overall structure as well as the sequencing and structure of the paragraphs. This capstone task involves evaluating the two pieces and arguing that one is more effective rhetorically than the other. The student essays will be published in a class anthology titled *Nature's Pilgrims*, with an introduction by the teacher. Each student receives a copy, and copies are placed in local public and school libraries for circulation. As a result, Paul and his students take particular care with the stages in the DWC, with the ultimate goal of producing not just *A* papers but publishable work for the entire community.

WHAT ASSIGNMENTS WILL ELICIT THE BEST STUDENT WRITING?

In the writing assignments described above, note that there is a variety of explanatory and argumentative tasks. By focusing on genre you teach a wide variety of language usage: language as story (the novel), language as ritual performance (drama), language as music (poetry), and so on. This approach leads organically to definition and description essays. Further, when students begin to dig deeper into the elements that define the various genres, they will be ready to write analysis, comparison, and evaluation essays involving much more sophisticated evaluations of the creative literature they are studying. When Adler and van Doren write in *How to Read a Book* that "beauty is harder to analyze than truth," they then go on to discuss how to analyze literary "beauty," by analyzing the elements that define various kinds of literature (1972, p. 204).

It's worth repeating that we include the personal essay in the realm of creative literature and argue that essays like "My Wood" (E. M. Forster) and "A Room of One's Own" (Virginia Woolf) or excerpts from longer nonfiction works (Thoreau and Dillard) are well worth studying because they can be analyzed for medium as well as message. Students can study the masters of expository writing as a way of improving their own prose. Finally, we believe that the DWC should result in publishable work from most—if not *all*—of your students, so we emphasize publication for an authentic audience that has a vested interest in the subject.

Writing from Experience and Opinion

Not all writing examines a text as closely or analytically as the essay, report, or critique does in the academic classroom. In order for students to develop skills in crafting descriptions, anecdotes, and narratives, students should learn to produce writing that engages readers in a more emotional and less formal manner than they do in academic writing. This requires students to learn to use language and structure differently than they do in more formal academic writing, although academic writing can benefit from an occasional anecdote or description. One way to think about this difference is that narrative and opinion writing depend on style as much as or more than content.

The goal of teaching narrative and opinion writing is to "engage and orient the reader" (National Governors Association Center for Best Practices & Council of Chief State School Officers, 2010a, p. 43). When writing narratives the goal is to engage readers by entertaining them in some way. When writing opinion or persuasive works, the goal is to engage readers by influencing them, often using emotional appeal. In both types of writing, logic and evidence-based reasoning are less important than the ability to use language and structure to create an effect.

The Common Core standards for writing narratives call for students to use "effective technique, descriptive details, and clear event sequences" such as dialogue and sensory detail as early as 3rd grade (National Governors Association Center for Best Practices & Council of Chief State School Officers, 2010a, p. 20). Opinion works, such as editorials, commentaries, and some blogs, also require skills in using techniques that make an emotional appeal in an effort to persuade the reader to at least "listen" to the author's point of view. In both nonfiction narrative and opinion writing, the ability to use language to draw the reader into the ideas expressed in the work demands that the writer understand how to choose language and pace and sequence the account in order to create an effect. We include this kind of writing in the language arts or English classroom because writing these types of assignment products largely involves teaching style over content. Nevertheless, other subject area teachers could give assignments that involve students in writing an account or interviewing someone about an event.

As in the writing lessons described in other chapters, the DWC writing lesson draws on texts and starts with a seminar. The seminar should revolve around a model text and help students understand the structure of the model text and the techniques used to produce this kind of text. The subsequent writing task could be a memoir, a feature article, an interview, an account of an event or historical person's experience, or, if you're bold enough, a script for a play or documentary.

Here are three assignment prompts in which students write in the narrative style. In each lesson, students analyze one or more texts to discern the voice, use of language, and sequencing typical of each type of text:

Upper Elementary: *Write a new ending to the Cherokee folktale "How the World Was Made" so that it complements the story and uses some of the same techniques.*

Middle School: *After reading letters from Civil War soldiers, write an account of life in a camp as if you were there. Include illustrations and visuals.*

High School: *After analyzing the structure of Flannery O'Connor's "A Good Man Is Hard to Find," write a short story in which you develop a plot line in which each event builds on the other to create a climax.*

Here are three samples in which students write opinion or persuasive works. In each case, students should analyze the structure, logic, and language of a model text during the seminar:

Upper Elementary: *Write a letter to a member of the school board in which you state your opinion about whether your school should keep the computer lab open during summer months. Be sure to provide data or other evidence for your position.*

Middle School: *After studying the experience of miners during the Gold Rush, write an editorial for the Sacramento Bee in which you argue for or against taxing the miners.*

High School: *Produce a script for a short documentary in which you identify a community problem and propose a solution. Follow the guidelines for submitting your work to the Teen Arts and Video Challenge.*

* * *

Ultimately, the goal of writing about literature is that your students become increasingly independent as readers, thinkers, and writers. One way to evaluate their cyclical experiences with writing is that over time they should internalize the DWC—the Discourse Sequence, the Transition to Writing Sequence, and the Writing Sequence—so that the stages become habitual. In this way, students not only learn the conceptual content from your course of study; they also learn the literacy tools they will need in high school and beyond.

 ## CHECK YOUR THINKING

What values would you identify for a seminar in your class? What text might you choose to engage students in thinking about those values? What writing prompt would you then assign?

See Appendix C (p. 162) for possible responses.

8

DWC in the History or Social Studies Classroom

Histories make men wise.

—Francis Bacon, *The Philosophical Works of Francis Bacon*

Writing in history or social studies class is different from writing about other subjects in two important ways. First, writing about history means writing about a special set of ideas that fall largely within the domain of the historian—*cause, change,* and *time,* to name only a few—or ideas that have traditionally become the subject of social and political scientists—*government, justice, law,* and the like. Second, writing about history often means practicing historical analysis and interpretation. Historical analysis, in turn, means attempting to understand past events from the point of view of those who lived through those events, not from our own distant perspective. The ability to understand the perspective of historical individuals and groups is often referred to as "historical thinking," and this kind of thinking is often what we must practice in order to discuss or write about the past.

Practicing the DWC in social studies class should be where students learn the art of historical thinking. As part of a national assessment effort called "The Nation's Report Card," the U.S. Department of Education developed benchmarks for student achievement in U.S. history.

Their rubric divides history learning into three basic dimensions: major historical themes, chronological periods, and ways of knowing and thinking about history. The third dimension is further divided into two parts: historical knowledge and perspective versus historical analysis and interpretation. These are important distinctions because they help define the conceptual curriculum in history: historical themes, perspective, and analysis and interpretation. By defining the conceptual history curriculum, these benchmark dimensions make it clear why we must teach both seminar discussion and writing in social studies classes. The only way for our students to truly think about history is by writing about it, and the only way for them to learn to think like historians is through discussing and writing about historical ideas. This conviction—that close reading, discourse, and writing are the proper business of history classes—is reinforced by the Common Core's emphasis on literacy skills in all disciplines.

WHAT IDEAS ARE WORTH TALKING AND WRITING ABOUT?

Close reading, discussion, and writing well are hard work. They require significant thought and effort in all three sequences of DWC: the Discourse Sequence, the Transition to Writing Sequence, and the Writing Sequence. For our students to be willing to put themselves through the paces of DWC, the subjects we address and the topics we assign should offer them something in return. The ideas that we address through discussion and writing should mean enough to our students that they are worth exploring over an extended period of time. If, for example, we use Mortimer Adler's 102 Great Ideas (1952) as a starting point, we discover a list of primary concepts that are native to the study of history: *cause, change, custom and convention, dialectic, history, memory and imagination, one and many, opposition, progress, time,* and *world.*

Beyond this initial list of primary concepts that deal with the development of human society over time, there is a secondary list of Great Ideas that are often studied in social studies class: *citizen, constitution, democracy, duty, equality, government, justice, labor, law, liberty, monarchy, oligarchy, revolution, slavery, state, tyranny, war and peace,* and *wealth.* These are examples (not an exhaustive list) of ideas worth thinking about—and therefore worth discussing and writing about. These ideas are also complex and ambiguous by nature, which means that they provide us as teachers with multiple opportunities for crafting compelling assignments. Finally, they provide our students with multiple perspectives from which to respond.

In sum, the study of history should include a focus on ideas—especially if we want our students to invest the time and energy it takes to think deeply and write well about events that, at first glance, may seem irrelevant because they are so distant in time and space.

Consider a social studies teacher named Angela who teaches Tennessee history in a rural middle school in eastern Tennessee. She is building a unit of study around the removal of the Cherokee Indians from their traditional lands in the 1830s. In discussions with other Tennessee history teachers and with colleagues at the National Paideia Center, she identified the following concepts as the curricular bedrock for her unit: *citizenship, constitution, democracy, property,* and *individual versus group.* She confessed that once she began to consider the possibilities, her problem was an embarrassment of riches, for this single topic in Tennessee history resonated with numerous evocative concepts. She knew her students were interested in issues of citizenship and the rights of the individual, so she planned to open her unit with a Paideia seminar discussion of these powerful ideas. In this way, she hoped to generate the student interest that would carry her class through the hard work of formal discussion and extended writing.

WHAT VOCABULARY IS WORTH TEACHING?

As discussed in Chapter 2, true fluency is developed through practice in speaking and listening as well as writing. One important element in fluency is vocabulary—not just the vocabulary that helps students excel on standardized tests but also the vocabulary that equips students to think about complex ideas. In building a literacy-based unit, teachers should be conscious of the general subject area vocabulary that can be taught as an organic part of that unit as well as specific vocabulary that students will need to read the texts under discussion, speak about them with growing familiarity, and write about them with confidence.

Angie teaches in a state that pays detailed attention to content area vocabulary in social studies as well as other subjects. In planning her unit on the Cherokee removal, she referred to the *Tennessee Academic Vocabulary: A Guide for Tennessee Educators*, produced by the Tennessee Department of Education (revised most recently in 2009). From the terms listed under the category of Tennessee History for 8th grade students, she chose four—*constitutional, diplomacy, domestic,* and *insurrection*—for inclusion in the glossary for her unit, adding them to the list of conceptual themes she'd already chosen. Working on the theory that content literacy meant, at least in part, mastery of content vocabulary, Angie planned to include these terms (along with others gleaned directly from the readings) on a classroom word wall and in a unit glossary that students would eventually draw from in their writing.

WHAT TEXTS ARE WORTH TALKING AND WRITING ABOUT?

The Common Core State Standards place a premium on writing about challenging nonfiction texts. In history, there are three types of texts that are generally worth the time and energy it requires for close reading and extended attention through discourse and writing:

- Primary sources from the historical period under consideration
- Secondary sources from the historical period but removed from the events
- Secondary sources by trained historians removed in time from the historical period

Primary sources include artifacts like government documents, speeches, letters by eyewitnesses, and transcripts, as well as nonverbal texts like photographs, maps, and cartoons. Secondary sources from the period include texts that were produced during the same historical period (and so shed light on the period) but may not provide credible information about a specific event, such as transcripts of speeches recorded from memory and accounts of events by participants or witnesses that are written down years later. Although these texts tell historians a great deal about the time and place as well as the individuals who created the record, they are not often as instructive as the primary sources concerning the same event. The third type of valuable texts is published histories—often written centuries later—by trained researchers whose work has been peer-reviewed through the publication process.

In planning her unit on the Cherokee removal, Angie knew from the start of the planning process which primary source she wanted for the central text: General Winfield Scott's "Orders No. 25," the published orders read to the U.S. troops describing how and why they were to round up and remove the Cherokee in 1838. Angie had used it successfully before as a seminar text and believed it would provide a good basis for an argumentative essay. She also identified two other texts she wanted to use as background for the unit. The first was a first-person memoir by a soldier (John Burnett) who participated in the removal, written down decades later on the occasion of his 80th birthday as a description and explanation for his children. The second was a useful excerpt in a 1988 history of the removal titled *Trail of Tears* by novelist and historian John Ehle, who was impeccable in his use of source materials. She believed that this modern narrative history would provide her students with the background they needed to put the historical events surrounding the removal of the Cherokee in perspective. She planned to focus on Winfield Scott's "Orders No. 25" as the primary text for close reading and seminar discourse and supplement the speech with appropriate excerpts from the two secondary texts.

WHAT ASSIGNMENTS WILL ELICIT THE BEST STUDENT WRITING?

Based on her planning to this point, Angie chose to construct her unit of study around the following writing task:

> *Did the U.S. government have the constitutional right to remove the Cherokee people from their ancestral lands by force? After reading General Winfield Scott's "Orders No. 25" and excerpts from Trail of Tears, write a fully developed essay in which you argue whether or not the government had the right to remove the Cherokee. Support your discussion with evidence from the texts.*

In her notes, she thought of this as an *argumentation-analysis* essay, based in part on the categories defined by the Literacy Design Collaborative. She also thought that in order to respond to this prompt, her students would have to analyze the primary text closely before writing about it, practicing analyzing and creating. She wanted her students to first read the "Orders" multiple times, adding vocabulary to their copies of the unit glossary, and then discuss the text in a formal seminar. She believed the "Orders" took her students into the human drama of the removal, including the struggle between individual rights and governmental control. She also believed that a close reading of the "Orders" would engage her students because they could see issues of citizenship, Constitution, democracy, and the role of the individual (her original thematic ideas) as they played out in the lives of ordinary people.

In *How to Read a Book*, Mortimer Adler and Charles van Doren argue that in reading a historical text, you must (1) define what a text is (by genre), (2) describe its structure, and (3) summarize its argument, before (4) finally being in a position to discuss its significance (1972). Angie had been careful all year to take her students through this process in responding to primary texts and had often given writing assignments early in the year that required her students to define, describe, and summarize short historical texts with great precision and care. She felt that in this case they were ready to go on to the next step and discuss the significance of General

Scott's "Orders" in detail while also drawing on Burnett's memoir and Ehle's modern narrative history. By the end of the year, she wanted her students to be writing well-constructed arguments referring to multiple texts.

Angie's practice suggests the kinds of writing assignments that can profitably be given in a social studies class: definition and analysis in an informational or explanatory format, leading in time to well-ordered argumentation that draws on multiple sources in support of a claim. It also suggests how wise teachers design their writing tasks with the entire syllabus in mind, building in a series of units of study that task students with increasingly demanding texts for reading and seminar discussion, leading to writing assignments of increasing rigor. It is important to note that Angie was emphatic about the careful use of the writing process by her students, working through each stage in the process with them on all her major assignments. In time, the students had come to trust and believe in the writing process—as time-consuming as it often was—because they saw their own writing growing consistently in quantity and sophistication. The students teased their teacher about running a secret seminar and writing laboratory rather than a Tennessee history class.

During both the Discourse and Writing Sequences in her Cherokee removal unit, Angie quoted Adler and van Doren to her students:

> It is possible that no kind of literature has greater effect on the actions of men than history. . . . History, which tells us of the actions of men of the past, often does lead us to make changes, to try to better our lot. . . . History suggests the possible, for it describes things that have already been done. If they have been done, perhaps they can be done again—or perhaps they can be avoided. (1972, p. 243)

"What can we learn?" she kept asking her students throughout the Discourse and Writing Sequences of the unit. "What can we learn from this text about the people who lived through these events in 1838? And what can we learn about ourselves?" What this teacher was seeking to accomplish with these nagging questions is an apt lesson for all history teachers.

Through the DWC, she was teaching both historical thinking (What can we learn from this text about the people who lived through these events in 1838?) and personal reflection (What can we learn about ourselves?). She was using discussion and writing to teach thinking.

Angie also sought to make talking and writing about history a relevant experience for her students by defining an authentic audience for each essay. In this particular case, she had engaged a high school history teacher and his advanced placement students to read the final drafts of her students' essays and score them using the same rubric they used to assess student papers in an advanced placement history course. In return, she and her Tennessee history students—along with parent volunteers—were hosting a reception at the middle school for the teacher and his students, where the high school teacher would comment in general on the middle school students' work (no names or specific references) and discuss how important writing was in high school, college, and beyond. Angie pitched this experience to her students as their opportunity to "do high school work" as middle school students and to be rewarded not just by a real-world assessment but also by the opportunity to talk about the high school experience with those who were immersed in it.

WHAT CHARACTERIZES THE BEST STUDENT WRITING IN HISTORY?

The best thinking and the best writing have three characteristics: They are clear, coherent, and sophisticated. Written clarity and coherence are basically consistent across subject areas; however, sophisticated writing in social studies class has a unique characteristic. In order to practice historical analysis and interpretation and write well about historical perspective, students need to be clear in their own minds about the various points of view they are describing and analyzing (both historical and modern) and juxtapose them as objectively as possible. To do this well, they must learn to suspend their own judgment in order to fully understand the multiple points of view of others so that they can write well about them. Learning to understand and manipulate various perspectives—including contradictory perspectives—is vital to historical thinking, and it is what students learn in seminar discussion.

A social studies teacher like Angie, then, knows that she has been successful in teaching her students to talk and write about history when their written products are clear, coherent, and sophisticated in analyzing the multiple points of view necessary to understand an historical concept.

CHECK YOUR THINKING

What are the "big ideas" that you build your units of study around? When and how do you use discussion and writing as a means for your students to practice historical thinking about those ideas?

See Appendix C (p. 162) for possible responses.

9

DWC in the Science and Math Classrooms

The more clearly we write, the more clearly we see and feel and think.

—Joseph Williams and Gregory G. Colomb, *Style*

Teaching writing involving science and math helps students clarify their thinking, examine key concepts in these subjects, and acquire ways of thinking specific to each discipline. Teaching students how to write documents common to these subject areas will prepare them for future work in these professions—both in college and beyond. Each discipline may have its own lexicon and protocols, but the production process outlined in the Discourse and Writing Cycle remains the same as for the humanities. Students will find many topics of interest to them in these disciplines as well as opportunities to produce other types of written products. Teachers in these subjects will find that the types of writing produced in science and math provide good opportunities for focusing on informative writing and the role of graphic material.

Professionals in these subjects write to document their work for peers and, at times, for the general public. As a result, students can both write in more traditional forms in order to sharpen their thinking and learn to write in the modes that are native to science and math. Scientists write, for example, to record experiments, ask for research money, and describe phenomena. Math has its own language, one based in numerals, but mathematicians also have to explain their reasoning in technical documents to peers and wider audiences. Those in engineering, manufacturing, and computer technologies often write manuals and reports in order to document work procedures and processes. Increasingly, these fields are integrated and require scientists to use math to explain data or engineers to explain technical concepts. As is often the case in science, a mathematical explanation may be necessary to explain some model or occurrence, so students also need skills in integrating math into prose. Writers in these subjects should communicate accurately and with precision.

WRITING TECHNICAL PRODUCTS

Ernest H. Williams discusses four common products in science, math, and technical writing in "Writing in the Sciences" (n.d.):

- The experimental report in science
- The response paper in science and math
- The research report in science
- The proposal in science, math, and other technical fields

Many scientists also learn to write technical articles designed to appeal to a general public. Besides assigning demands similar to those in these fields, you can ask students to format their products as memos or use other workplace formats including data, graphs, or math symbols and computations.

Each type of technical writing is distinguished by a set of traits specific to a purpose and audience (Olson, 2013; Williams, n.d.). The science report involves a lab or experimental process; requires a specific structure that involves a claim, evidence, and results; and is substantiated by reasoning. The response paper addresses a theory, a concept, or a response to a problem or research. Science and technical journalists write nonfiction narratives to better inform the general public about a scientific, mathematical, or technical topic. All products, however, should share two common features: they (1) are grounded in fact and (2) mirror the types of assignments students will encounter in high school and college coursework or professional settings. Middle school teachers in science, math, and technical subjects should distribute writing assignments among the different types. Since elementary teachers often teach all four core subjects, they should distribute writing assignments among the core subjects in order to expose students to a variety of writing situations while keeping writing assignments manageable. Depending on the grade or skill level of your students, set expectations requiring less or more information, explanation, or discourse. Even in elementary grades, students can understand the need to include specific traits in their products and relate these to a scientific or mathematical purpose and audience.

WRITING IN SCIENCE

Science as a discipline is concerned with a large number of concepts that all but demand rigorous reading, discussion, and writing on the part of students—if they are to be understood. In addition to the overarching idea of science as a way of interpreting the world, consider the following from Adler's Great Ideas (1952): *astronomy, change, element, evolution, hypothesis, induction, matter, nature, physics, sign and symbol, space, time,* and *universal and particular*. These ideas are embedded in the classic texts of science, so one of the best ways to access them in the classroom is through the DWC. Teachers can craft assignments that open the world of scientific thought to their students and then ask students to respond in writing— through the more common forms of written products as well as types more often associated with science as a discipline.

A number of high school science teachers that we work with introduce scientific thought through a literacy cycle based on the classic definition of *induction* from Isaac Newton's *Optics* (see Chapter 10 for the full DWC on this text). Through close reading, discussion, and writing, students come in contact with one of the most important minds in the history of science, defining how and why science looks at the world differently than any other discipline (except perhaps mathematics). They wrestle with the ideas of hypothesis, induction, and the universal and particular—all while practicing the communication and thinking skills required by 21st century life.

In addition to the more standard written tasks we require of middle and high school students, science teachers can and should vary their assignments to include the products that scientists themselves often produce.

The Lab Report

The lab report documents an experiment and requires a basic format in which students state a hypothesis, a review of methods, a discussion of results, and a conclusion. Other sections might include acknowledgments and literature cited. This kind of report is used not only in science but also in engineering and any field where experiments are conducted. The experimental report is essentially an investigative and analytical work requiring students to document a process as well as analyze results. The teaching of writing involved in this assignment should focus on the purpose of the document and the resulting organization of ideas. This product offers good opportunities to teach reasoning and logic, since the construct of an experimental procedure is all about testing an idea.

Another opportunity offered by the lab report is the role of formatting devices, such as bulleting and headings, in order to help readers discern hierarchies of statements, particularly when delineating a process. Teaching a lab report involves helping students not only manage the writing of a process in a specific format but also acquire skills in precision and accuracy: for example, stating a process in sufficient detail or translating a data set accurately. You have an opportunity to teach thinking that will make the difference between a "sloppy" scientist or technician and one who can communicate work clearly to others, a key function in these fields. The following are strategies to help you teach students to write with clarity and precision in experimental reports.

- Teach the formats for the various parts of your template and how they differ, particularly the difference between "results" and "conclusion."
- Work with students to identify discipline-specific vocabulary relevant to the experiment and field.
- Teach the use of formal language to establish an appropriate tone for a technical report.

The Response Paper

The response paper is a reflective composition, a cousin of the essay, in which the writer thinks about some phenomenon or concept with the purpose of sharing this thinking with peers. These tasks are not full-blown research papers but, instead, ask students to explore their own thoughts about a core concept or idea.

- Teach ways to establish a tone that explores, examines, questions, or muses about a topic, idea, or phenomena, using language that is less technical but not too informal.
- Point out and demonstrate the proper use of the "I" voice in these types of compositions.
- Teach how to include a competing argument or data to develop a "point, counterpoint" discourse.

Sample prompts for a response paper include the following:

- *Science: What would the world be like without a sun? Write an essay in which you imagine such a world and explain the science behind it.*
- *Science/technical subject: Would robots make learning easier or harder? Write a response paper in which you explore both possibilities.*

The Research Report

The research report requires students in science and technical subjects to examine or argue some aspect of the topic after reading multiple texts and sources. It is essentially a synthesis paper for which they read multiple texts and organize what they have read into a report. The research report assignment can seem overwhelming. Keep the topic or question narrow in order to focus your instruction on how researchers choose, use, and embed evidence for their claims or theses. In addition to the DWC demands, the structural demands for the research report involve the following:

- An abstract or summary often appears first in order to give the reader the main points of the report, including any overall finding
- A review of the literature in the opening section
- Headings to distinguish parts of the development of the report

Sample assignment prompts for reports include the following:

- *What is nanotechnology, and what are its potential uses? Write a research report that addresses the question, and discuss whether the science and technology is useful.*
- *Write a research report for your supervisor in which you argue for the need for recycling.*

The Proposal

Many professionals will at some time in their careers write proposals to acquire revenue for their work. Proposals can be long and involved documents, but students can learn the basics, even in middle school. A proposal is the business version of an argumentative essay in that its purpose is to convince the reader to support a project. Often, proposals are written by more than one person, so this assignment creates opportunities for group writing.

A proposal should contain an appeal that points to a desired outcome. Professionals write proposals to fund projects that would lead to a better understanding of some phenomenon or condition. Proposals are common in business, particularly to fund start-up businesses or expansions, and you can find proposal guidelines and forms at your local business store. The common features of a proposal include the following:

- A summary that highlights the appeal, impact, and the project's product or outcome
- An appeal stated in concise terms and dollars (opening and claim)

- A rationale for the project (need or problem and solution) and its impact or utility (development)
- A description of the project, including materials, staff, timeline (development)
- A budget that reflects the costs of the project description and supports the purpose of the request (development)
- Impact restated (closing)

Sample assignment prompts for proposals include the following:

- *You have a great idea for a science project and are seeking revenues from the Parent-Teacher Association for a grant. Write a proposal and attach a budget.*
- *Your science experiment shows potential for saving the school vegetable garden from a local infestation of beetles. Write a grant to a community funder to acquire funds to address the problem to save the garden.*

The Manual

Technical writing often involves writing manuals for professional audiences as well as a general audience. Writing an effective, user-friendly manual requires a thorough understanding of the audience. If the manual is written for a novice user or the general public, for example, the manual may need illustrations. If it is written for peers or other technicians, it may need fewer illustrations but could include more detailed explanations. To make a manual user-friendly, students should consider layout and formatting in order to convey their information. Your instruction should involve the following:

- Demonstrations and analyses of the role of layout and illustrations.
- Techniques for writing concisely while providing all necessary information or process steps. In a manual, more words are sometimes clearer than fewer words. An activity that forces conciseness asks students to write a summary several times by hand. By the final copy, they most likely will have eliminated unnecessary words or sentences.

- Prioritizing and organizing information chronologically—by steps or stages—or from most important to least important. Ask students to work in small groups to determine order of events or processes.

Sample assignments for a manual product in science include the following:

  - *Develop and write cooking directions for the general public that explain how to cook a traditional dish of your choice.*
  - *Write and illustrate a manual performing an experiment to test soil for growing a garden.*
  - *As a class, we are to write a chemistry lab manual for our school. Your job is to write _____ (a section) of the chemistry lab manual to include explanations about the scientific process and safety tips.*

The Descriptive Paper

Assigning a descriptive paper can widen the range of writing situations in science, math, and technical coursework. The descriptive paper is a journalistic product that considers a nonprofessional audience and is often published in a magazine or local newspaper. Assigning a descriptive paper can give you and your students a break from more formal writing assignments and provide opportunities to translate technical material into accessible language.

This kind of writing requires students to use both narrative and expository strategies. The writer uses descriptive language alongside the discipline's more formal language to help the lay reader understand the composition's subject. Students should aim to balance a narrative style with professional accuracy. For mathematicians to explain some aspect of Euclid's theory to a general audience, they present not only the proof but also enough explanation for the reader to grasp its significance. This balancing act was cleverly done in the popular television series *Numbers,* in which three mathematicians helped the FBI solve crimes and explained probability and other theories to the viewer as they worked through their reasoning.

Consider this opening passage about dark matter: "If you look at the sky on a clear night, you can see a few thousand stars. With a telescope you can see a lot more—distant galaxies, gas clouds, and dust between the stars. All of this stuff either gives off light or absorbs it. Indeed, if stars didn't give off light, we wouldn't know they were there" (Trefil, 1996, p. 83). The author employs both the language of science and common speech language to engage readers' attention and to explain the phenomenon.

To teach students to write for a wider audience while staying true to the discipline, consider the following instructional strategies:

- Have students read and analyze how professional authors use narrative language to describe a scientific or technical feature, event, or function.
- Have students analyze professional articles for structure and stylistic devices.
- Use peer review (student-to-student) to help students gauge whether language choices are illustrative while also conveying the science or technology involved in the composition.

Sample assignment prompts include the following:

- *Write an article for the school newspaper in which you describe what natural forces cause a tornado.*
- *Write an article for a younger audience in which you explain how and why a volcano erupts and the science behind it.*
- *Write a feature article for a science magazine in which you explain a technological invention of some importance and how that invention has changed the way we work, play, or function in our lives.*
- *Write a manual detailing how to build a pendulum.*

WRITING IN MATH

Just as with science, mathematics is built on a structure of ideas. Because of this, all truly successful students know how to think about math concepts as well as apply those concepts in the practical world. Consider again Adler's (1952) Great Ideas, where you find not just *mathematics* itself as concept but also the following: *form, infinity, logic, one and many, quality, quantity, reasoning, relation,* and *sign and symbol.*

Any good math teacher will tell you, however, that this list barely scratches the conceptual surface of the discipline. A math teacher in an urban Paideia middle school has constructed an entire literacy cycle around the idea of zero and the powerful role it plays in almost all mathematical operations. Just as it would be a mistake to teach science or history without teaching the foundational ideas of those subjects, it is equally mistaken to teach math without teaching students how to think conceptually about its fundamental ideas.

Further, just as in science, the classic texts in math also embody the major concepts that shape the discipline. One high school geometry teacher that we work with begins each year with a DWC based on the first 23 definitions from Euclid's *Elements*. Although some math teachers would argue that Euclidean geometry is no longer valid, as our thinking about mathematical space has evolved, a quick review of this text reveals that these definitions still form the foundation of basic geometry. The teacher who developed this literacy cycle argues that her students are not only learning core mathematical concepts through discussion and writing but also learning to *think* like mathematicians.

Even so, some educators question whether seminar discussion followed by intensive writing is an appropriate way to teach math. Perhaps the simplest way to address this question is to examine the Common Core's Standards for Mathematical Practice, as they are representative of the best in contemporary thinking about math instruction. Of the eight standards, the first three are clearly related to formal classroom discussion (National Governors Association Center for Best Practices & Council of Chief State School Officers, 2010b, p. 6):

1. Make sense of problems and persevere in solving them.
2. Reason abstractly and quantitatively.
3. Construct viable arguments and critique the reasoning of others.

Furthermore, within the third standard, the detailed description all but demands the practice of classroom discussion:

Mathematically proficient students understand and use stated assumptions, definitions, and previously established results in constructing arguments. They make conjectures and build a logical progression of statements to explore the truth of their conjectures. . . . They justify their conclusions, communicate them to others, and respond to the arguments of others. . . . Mathematically proficient students are also able to compare the effectiveness of two plausible arguments, distinguish correct logic or reasoning from that which is flawed, and—if there is a flaw in an argument—explain what it is. . . . Students at all grades can listen or read the arguments of others, decide whether they make sense, and ask useful questions to clarify or improve the arguments. (National Governors Association Center for Best Practices & Council of Chief State School Officers, 2010b, pp. 6–7)

It is difficult to imagine a math classroom that successfully teaches this important standard without consistent use of student discussion followed by student writing. Of the other five standards, at least three would also come into play in math seminars: "Model with mathematics," "Look for and make use of structure," "Look for and express regularity in repeated reasoning" (2010b, pp. 6–7). Once math teachers grasp the power of the DWC to teach these standards, we have found that they respond as enthusiastically as the rest of the faculty to the use of discourse-infused units that feature close reading, formal discussion, and extensive writing. Below are sample prompts involving math students in explaining a concept or practice:

- *Write for a younger audience an explanation of "zero" and discuss how it is used in math (similar process for other math concepts, such as negative numbers, fractions, etc.).*
- *Re-create a chapter or section from the math textbook while you work in groups to describe a mathematical concept or process in your own words and then provide both your own examples and problem sets.*
- *Write a process analysis report in which you analyze a mathematical formula and then explain in detail how to use that formula to solve a series of problems.*

WRITING IN TECHNICAL SUBJECTS

Despite some perceptions that writing isn't necessary for students aspiring to work in technical fields, writing is a critical skill if they are to manage the demands of the technical workplace. Writing tasks ranging from bids, proposals, manuals, and documentation are common in engineering, construction, and the computer fields. If you are a science, math, or technical subject teacher, assigning writing assignments enables your students to acquire several critical skills, including vocabulary, reasoning, and content relevant to your discipline. Writing helps students learn and also prepares them for the real world in which they must adapt their writing to specific purposes and situations. As one educator recently pointed out, "Writing is cash." Those who have acquired the skills and practice to write for a variety of purposes are better positioned to produce the proposals, reports, manuals, and trade articles that make them college-ready and, later, invaluable employees in the workplace.

CHECK YOUR THINKING

Often assignments in these fields are interdisciplinary. What would it involve in your school if two teachers taught an assignment together? Review the following sample interdisciplinary assignment prompts and think about what roles each discipline might play:

- *Science and math: Conduct an experiment in which you determine the chemical reaction when you combine any set of the three selected liquids. Write a lab report and include an explanation for each reaction.*
- *Engineering and language arts: After participating in the seminar on bridges, conduct an experiment to determine the highest level of stress a bridge made of cardboard paper can withstand. Write a report detailing your experiment and your conclusion.*
- *Mechanics and technology: Your lawn mower is costing you too much money to run. Write a short memo in which you determine which fuel is more efficient and document your process and findings.*

See Appendix C (p. 162) for possible responses.

10

DWC Lesson Plans for Elementary, Middle, and High School

In this chapter, we provide detailed DWC lessons for elementary, middle, and high school students. Each lesson starts with a Discourse Sequence, which leads in turn through the Transition to Writing and Writing Sequences. We have provided student writing artifacts with three* of the lesson plans.

These specific DWC lesson plans were developed by the National Paideia Center and emphasize the full literacy cycle, beginning with close reading strategies (under "Pre-Seminar Content") and followed by the discussion and writing strategies emphasized in this book. You can find a wide variety of these DWC lesson plans for K–12 classrooms at www .paideia.org/teachers/seminar-lesson-plans/. You can also find and construct similar plans at www.ldc.org.

Upper Elementary Grades
"Thorn Rose, the Sleeping Beauty" by the Brothers Grimm (language arts) 12× Multiplication Table (math)*

Middle Grades
"How the World Was Made," Cherokee Folktale (social studies)*
Geological Map of Oklahoma (science)

High School Grades
From *Optics* by Sir Isaac Newton (science)
"Body Ritual Among the Nacirema" by Horace Miner (language arts)*

"THORN ROSE, THE SLEEPING BEAUTY"
BY THE BROTHERS GRIMM

Grade/subject: Elementary school/language arts
Ideas, values: Choice, fate, language, magic, time

Pre-Seminar Content

- **Launch activity:** Define the terms *fate* versus *choice*. Write a brief sketch in which you describe a time in your life when you chose for yourself and a second sketch in which "fate" controlled what happened to you.
- **Inspectional read:** Distribute the text and ask participants to anticipate what they expect this reading to be like. Note genre, structure, and so on. Discuss what a folktale is. Have the students number the paragraphs in their copies of the text. Read the text for a first time aloud. Have participants identify any unfamiliar words or phrases.
- **Background:** Share that Jacob (1785–1863) and Wilhelm Grimm (1786–1859) were German academics, linguists, cultural researchers, lexicographers, and authors who together collected and published folklore. They are among the best-known storytellers of folktales, popularizing stories such as "Cinderella," "Hansel and Gretel," and "Snow White." Their first collection of folktales, *Children's and Household Tales*, was published in 1812.

- **Vocabulary development:** Discuss the unfamiliar vocabulary words until all participants are comfortable with their meaning. Remember to include the following terms in your discussion: *folktale, fate,* and *choice.*
- **Analytical read:** Assign individual or groups of students a role through which to view the story (e.g., king, queen, Wise Women, Thorn Rose, various princes). Read the story aloud a second time while the students take notes on what their assigned characters must have felt or thought at various points in the story. Then have the individuals or groups share out their insights while the entire class takes notes on their copies of the text.

Pre-Seminar Process

- Define and state purpose for Paideia seminar.
- Describe the responsibilities of facilitator and participants.
- Have participants set a personal goal.
- Agree on a group goal.

Seminar Discussion

Opening (identify main ideas from the text):

- Whose fault is it that Thorn Rose is forced to sleep for 100 years? (round-robin response)
- Based on the text, why is that character at fault? (spontaneous discussion)

Core (analyze textual details):

- What role do the 13 Wise Women play in this tale? Are they wise? Why or why not?
- Why do you think that the princess in this story is named Thorn Rose? Why not Rose Thorn?

- Is the prince who frees Thorn Rose (and the other inhabitants of the castle) a better prince or a better man than the others who had tried to break through? How do you know?
- What role does time play in this folktale?
- Does Thorn Rose do anything to cause her 100-year sleep or to wake herself up?

Closing (personalize and apply the textual ideas):

- Based on this story, do you believe that individuals choose what happens to them or that fate decides? Describe a time in your life when either choice or fate controlled what happened to you.

Post-Seminar Process

- Have participants write a self-assessment of their personal participation goal.
- Do a group assessment of the social and intellectual goals of seminar.
- Note reminders for next seminar.

Post-Seminar Content

- **Transition to writing:** Have participants take notes to brainstorm ideas that they heard, read, and thought during the seminar related to the ideas of fate and choice.
- **Writing task:** What role does fate play in "Thorn Rose, the Sleeping Beauty"? After reading "Thorn Rose, the Sleeping Beauty" by the Brothers Grimm, write an essay for fairy tale fans in which you identify the role of "fate" and argue whether or not it controls what happens to Thorn Rose. Give at least three

examples from the text to support your opinion. (argumentation/ identify-argue, LDC Task #A4)

- **Brainstorm:** Invite participants to talk in pairs for two minutes to share thoughts about what the writing task is asking.
- **Structuring the writing:** Allot a few minutes for all to sketch an outline for their writing. Remind students to use the outlining process to refine their thinking.
- **First draft:** Challenge all to draft their essay by listing key points. Refer to the original text in order to provide examples.
- **Collaborative revision:** Have participants work in pairs to read their first drafts aloud to each other, with emphasis on reader as creator and editor. Listener says back one point he or she heard clearly and asks one question for clarification. Have students switch roles. Give time for full revisions, resulting in a second draft.
- **Edit:** Once the second draft is complete, have participants work in groups of three or four, this time taking turns reading each other's second drafts slowly and silently, marking any spelling or grammar errors they find. (Have dictionaries and grammar handbooks available for reference.) Take this opportunity to clarify or reteach any specific grammar strategies you have identified your students needing. Give time for full revisions, resulting in a third and final draft.
- **Publish:** Publish the final copies of the resulting essays in a collection to be circulated through the school and local public libraries and used for exemplars for next year's class. Include the original version of "Thorn Rose, the Sleeping Beauty" as translated by Wanda Gág.

Note: This translation from the original German is by artist, writer, and translator Wanda Gág and can be found in her *More Tales from Grimm* (1947).

12× MULTIPLICATION TABLE

Grade/subject: Elementary school/mathematics
Ideas, values: Mathematics, form, pattern, quantity

Pre-Seminar Content

- **Launch activity:** Have participants read the poem "Arithmetic" by Carl Sandburg (www.poemhunter.com/poem/arithmetic/) and discuss how they (individually and collectively) think about numbers and arithmetic. Create a class poem (based on "Arithmetic") that captures funny ways of thinking about numbers, especially patterns in numbers.
- **Inspectional read:** Have participants examine the text as a table of numbers and list as many different patterns as they see. Discuss "even" and "odd" numbers and examine the table for further patterns in that context.
- **Background:** Share as developmentally appropriate: Multiplication (often denoted by the cross symbol "×" or by the absence of symbol) is the third basic mathematical operation of arithmetic, the others being addition, subtraction, and division (division is the fourth one, because it requires multiplication to be defined).
- **Vocabulary development:** Discuss any mathematical terms that you as facilitator or the students as participants will need in the discussion. Also note any math vocabulary that you want students to master as part of this experience (*integer, product, multiple,* etc.). Note that the result of a multiplication is called a product. A product of integers is a multiple of each factor. For example, 15 is the product of 3 and 5, and is both a multiple of 3 and a multiple of 5.
- **Analytical read:** Divide the class into pairs (perhaps assigning your "best" math students into different pairs so as to distribute expertise) and assign one integer (1–12) to each pair at random. Ask each pair to explore the table for that number and identify

any patterns they discover. Have each pair share insights in the order of the numbers themselves, that is, beginning with 1 and going as high as 12.

Pre-Seminar Process

- Define and state purpose for Paideia seminar.
- Describe the responsibilities of facilitator and participants.
- Have participants set a personal goal.
- Agree on a group goal.

Seminar Discussion

Opening (identify main ideas from the text):

- What is the most important pattern that you see in this table? (round-robin response)
- Why is that pattern important? (spontaneous discussion)

Core (analyze textual details):

- This table ends with the integer 12 (as in $12 \times 12 = 144$). Would adding more numbers (13, 14, 15, etc.) make a better table? Why or why not?
- Would adding a row and a column for zero ("0") make a better table? What would the answers or "products" be for the zero column/row? (i.e., $0 \times 1 = ?$)
- Using a ruler or other straightedge, draw a diagonal line from the "$\times$" in the upper left-hand corner to the number "144" in the lower right. Can you describe the pattern that explains the numbers on this line (1, 4, 9, 16, etc.)? What would be the next number on this line if you extended it?
- What other mathematical operations could we create a table for (addition, subtraction, division, etc.)? What would that table look like?

Closing (personalize and apply the textual ideas):

- What is your favorite number between 1 and 12? According to this table, what kinds of things does your favorite number do when it is multiplied by other numbers? Is there a pattern?

OR

- When do you need to use multiplication to help you understand things around you? How would this chart help you do that?

Post-Seminar Process

- Have participants write a self-assessment of their personal participation goal.
- Do a group assessment of the social and intellectual goals of seminar.
- Note reminders for next seminar.

Post-Seminar Content

- **Transition to writing:** Divide the class into two groups and assign each group the task of creating a similar table for addition or subtraction—using chart paper to display their results.
- **Writing task:** How do you use a mathematical table? After reading and discussing the "12× Multiplication Table," write a paragraph in which you explain to other elementary students how to use a mathematical table (either addition or subtraction). Refer to the appropriate table in your explanation. (informational or explanatory/explain, LDC Task #1E3)
- **Brainstorm:** Invite participants to talk in their two groups (addition and subtraction) for up to five minutes to share thoughts about what the writing task is asking and how they might respond.

- **Structuring the writing:** Allot a few minutes for all students to sketch an outline for their writing. Draft the outline and use it to refine their thinking. Provide students with an outline template or templates as necessary to "scaffold" this stage—keeping in mind that half the students will be writing about the addition table and the other half about the subtraction table.
- **First draft:** Challenge all to draft their explanations by listing key points about the appropriate table. Refer to the appropriate table in detail in order to illustrate key points. (At this point, discuss with the two groups the vocabulary they might need in order to clearly explain the process for using each table. Add these terms to math word wall.)
- **Collaborative revision:** Have participants work in pairs (one student from addition group with one student from subtraction group) to read their first drafts aloud to each other, with emphasis on reader as creator and editor. The listeners respond with one point they heard clearly and ask one question for clarification. Have students switch roles. Give time for full revisions, resulting in a second draft.
- **Edit:** Once the second draft is complete, have participants work in the same pairs (as in the revision stage) and this time take turns reading each other's second drafts slowly and silently, marking any spelling or grammar errors they find. (Have dictionaries and grammar handbooks available for reference.) Take this opportunity to clarify or reteach any specific grammar strategies you have identified as a need. Give time for full revisions, resulting in a third and final draft.
- **Publish:** Post the three tables (addition, subtraction, multiplication) in large size on a Math Wall in the classroom or hallway. Display student introductions and explanations in proximity to the addition and subtraction tables (see Figure 10.1).

Figure 10.1

Subtraction Table Student Exemplar

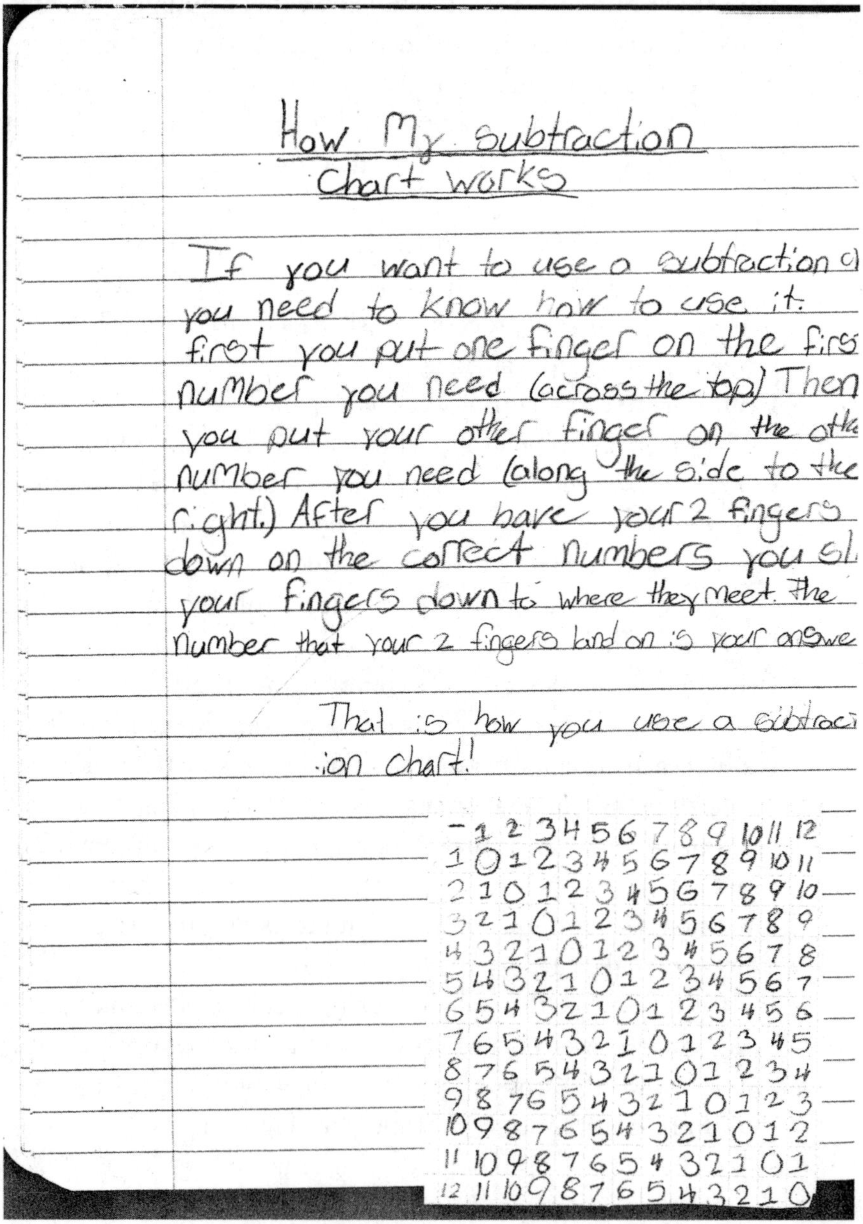

How My subtraction
Chart works

If you want to use a subtraction a
you need to know how to use it.
first you put one finger on the firs
number you need (across the top) Then
you put your other finger on the othe
number you need (along the side to the
right.) After you have your 2 fingers
down on the correct numbers you sl
your fingers down to where they meet. The
number that your 2 fingers land on is your answe

That is how you use a subtraci
ion chart!

```
 - 1  2  3  4  5  6  7  8  9  10 11 12
 1  0  1  2  3  4  5  6  7  8  9  10 11
 2  1  0  1  2  3  4  5  6  7  8  9  10
 3  2  1  0  1  2  3  4  5  6  7  8  9
 4  3  2  1  0  1  2  3  4  5  6  7  8
 5  4  3  2  1  0  1  2  3  4  5  6  7
 6  5  4  3  2  1  0  1  2  3  4  5  6
 7  6  5  4  3  2  1  0  1  2  3  4  5
 8  7  6  5  4  3  2  1  0  1  2  3  4
 9  8  7  6  5  4  3  2  1  0  1  2  3
10  9  8  7  6  5  4  3  2  1  0  1  2
11 10  9  8  7  6  5  4  3  2  1  0  1
12 11 10  9  8  7  6  5  4  3  2  1  0
```

HOW THE WORLD WAS MADE," CHEROKEE FOLKTALE

Grade/subject: Middle school/social studies
Ideas, values: Creation, culture, evolution, nature, story

Pre-Seminar Content

- **Launch activity:** Read the story aloud to students while they listen with several blank sheets of paper in front of them. Ask them to make a list of all the things (including animals) that are in the Cherokee world. During a second reading, have them sketch the world as the Cherokee saw it while you read. After you have finished reading the story, have students switch to a second sheet of paper and make a second draft of their sketches (because the world changes during the course of the story). Have the students break up into groups of three or four to share their sketches and discuss how they are alike and different.

- **Inspectional read:** Distribute the text to students and have them examine it without "reading" it. Discuss the nature of a folktale and what it means that James Mooney "collected" it. Have students number the paragraphs (1–7) in their copies of the text.

- **Background:** Share as appropriate: James Mooney (1861–1921) was born and grew up in Indiana. His formal education was limited to the public schools of the city. He became a self-taught expert on American Indian tribes through his own studies and his careful observation during long residences with different groups, including the Cherokee. Mooney was recognized as a national expert on the American Indian.

- **Vocabulary development:** Divide the class into two groups. Give one group green highlighters and the second group yellow highlighters. Read the story aloud (for the second time) while Group A (yellow) highlights all of the Cherokee words and Group B (green) highlights any other unfamiliar terms (including *cardinal points, vault, conjurer, fast, go to water, pray to their* *medicine,* etc.). Have the two groups work together to define their terms (Group A = Cherokee, Group B = other terms) and then share aloud for the whole class. Note: provide definitions for the phrases "go to water" (a purifying ritual involving immersing oneself in a cold mountain stream after prayer) and "pray to their medicine" (a form of prayer honoring one's personal nature).

- **Analytical read:** Divide the class up into pairs. Assign two or three pairs to create a large-scale drawing of the world according to the Cherokee (on the largest poster paper available)—using the best of the sketches from the launch activity. Assign one character (animals and plants as well as humans) to each of the other pairs and ask them to create a drawing of that character. Explain that, when completed, each of the characters will be posted on the picture of the world created by the first pairs. Work on the drawings for a specified period of time, noting that the students will be allowed to complete the drawings after the seminar.

Pre-Seminar Process

- Define and state purpose for Paideia seminar.
- Describe the responsibilities of facilitator and participants.
- Have participants set a personal goal.
- Agree on a group goal.

Seminar Discussion

Opening (identify main ideas from the text):

- Who do you think is the most important character in this story—out of all the animals, plants, and humans? (round-robin response)
- Why is that character so important? (spontaneous discussion)

Core (analyze textual details):

- Why does the Cherokee country remain full of mountains to this day?

- How do the Cherokee know that there is another world under this one (paragraph 5)?
- How does the Cherokee world evolve during the history of its creation? What do these changes teach us about the world?
- According to the text, what do the Cherokee not know about their world? Why do you think they are careful to include what "no one remembers" and "what we do not know"?
- Who is most important in the world of the Cherokee: animals, plants, or humans? How do you know?

Closing (personalize and apply the textual ideas):

- Would you like to live in the Cherokee world? Why or why not? If so, which character would you be?

Post-Seminar Process

- Have participants write a self-assessment of their personal participation goal.
- Do a group assessment of the social and intellectual goals of seminar.
- Note reminders for next seminar.

Post-Seminar Content

- **Transition to writing:** Have the students return to the drawings that they created during the analytical reading stage and work in their original pairs to add any new details (color, etc.) to the drawings. Then have them work together as a whole group to assemble those drawings into one large, coherent picture of the Cherokee world. Post the assembled world on the wall of the classroom or in the hallway outside the classroom.
- **Writing task:** Who is the most important character in the Cherokee tale "How the World Was Made"? After reading and discussing "How the World Was Made," write a full paragraph identifying the most important character and explain that

character's significance. Support your case with evidence from the text. (argumentation/analysis, LDC Task #A3)

- **Brainstorm:** Invite participants to talk in pairs for two minutes to share thoughts about what the writing task is asking.

- **Structuring the writing:** Allot a few minutes for all to write down a list of details they want to include in their paragraphs. Have students draft an outline for their writing and refine their thinking.

- **First draft:** Challenge all to draft their paragraphs by starting with a clear topic sentence and at least 10 sentences that give examples from the tale in support. Refer to the original text in order to illustrate key points.

- **Collaborative revision:** Have participants work in pairs to read their first drafts aloud to each other, with emphasis on reader as creator and editor. The listeners say back one point they heard clearly and ask one question for clarification. Have students switch roles. Give time for full revisions, resulting in a second draft.

- **Edit:** Once the second draft is complete, have participants work in groups of three or four, this time taking turns reading each other's second drafts slowly and silently, marking spelling or grammar errors they find, with a limit of five per paragraph. (Have dictionaries and grammar handbooks available for reference.) Take this opportunity to clarify or reteach any specific grammar strategies you have identified your students needing. Give time for full revisions and editing, resulting in a third and final draft (see student exemplar in Figure 10.2).

- **Publish:** Post the student paragraphs along with the large-scale portrait they created of the Cherokee world. Position the paragraphs close to the characters they describe and connect the paragraphs to the characters with string. Take a picture of the finished "world." Send both the photo and copies of the student paragraphs, with a cover letter from the class, to the Museum of the Cherokee Indian (589 Tsali Blvd, Cherokee, NC 28719) for the museum reference library.

Note: This story is drawn from *Myths of the Cherokee,* collected by James Mooney, Nineteenth Annual Report of the Bureau of American Ethnology 1897–1898, Part I (1900).

Figure 10.2

"How the World Was Made" Student Exemplar

"Cherokee world" Post-Seminar

I Believe the Dâyuni'sï or the water-beetle is the most important character, because he was the one who made the earth. The water beetle dove down into the water and pulled out soft mud. The mud then grew and dried. In the text it says "Then it dived to the bottom and came up with some soft mud, wich began to grow and spread. on every side until it became the island which we call earth." It was afterword Fastened to the sky with four cords". So if the water-beetle hadn't brought up mud to dry the earth wouldn't exist. If the water-beetle never pulled up mud to dry the great buzzard never could have mad mountians and valleys. If the water-beetle never brought up mud to dry the conjurers never would of brought the sun seven hand breaths high. Nothing would have happened on earth Benjemen Franklin wouldn't have even invented electricty.

THE GEOLOGICAL MAP OF OKLAHOMA

Grade/subject: Middle school/science
Ideas, values: Geology, region, science, sign and symbol

Pre-Seminar Content

- **Launch activity:** Write in your journal (or other format) a brief entry (~200 words) in which you describe Oklahoma as a state to someone from the other side of the country who has never visited.
- **Inspectional read:** Distribute the map and ask participants to anticipate what they expect to learn from a close examination of this text. Note any unexpected elements, such as color and so on.
- **Background:** Share that geologic maps, like all maps, are designed to show where things are. But, whereas the maps we know best show the distribution of roads or rivers or county boundaries, a geologic map shows the distribution of geologic features, including different kinds of rocks and faults. A geologic map is usually printed on top of a regular map (called a base map) to help you locate yourself on the map. The base map is printed with light colors so it doesn't interfere with seeing the geologic features on the map. The geology is represented by colors, lines, and special symbols unique to geologic maps. The oldest preserved geologic map is the Turin Papyrus, made around 1150 BC to identify gold deposits in Egypt.
- **Vocabulary development:** Divide the class into 13 groups and assign each group a geologic term from the list of geologic ages and types of rocks underneath the "panhandle" in the map's legend.
- **Analytical read:** Have the groups share their definitions, and then have the entire class work together to place the various "ages" on a time line for comparison. Display the time line prominently in the classroom for ready reference during the seminar.

Pre-Seminar Process

- Define and state purpose for Paideia seminar.
- Describe the responsibilities of facilitator and participants.
- Have participants set a personal goal.
- Agree on a group goal.

Seminar Discussion

Opening (identify main ideas from the text):

- What is the single most interesting detail you see on this map? (round-robin response)
- What makes that detail interesting? (spontaneous discussion)

Core (analyze textual details):

- Who do you think would use this map? How and why would they use it?
- What patterns do you see on this map? What do you think those patterns mean?
- How do you think what is "under the earth" is related to what we see on "top of the earth"?
- Using the types of rocks or landforms recorded on this map, can you divide the state into "natural" regions? If so, how?
- Geology is the "study of the earth's crust." Why do you think we have a whole science related just to the crust of the earth?
- Based on the geology of Oklahoma, how would you divide the state into regions? Why?

Closing (personalize and apply the textual ideas):

- If you were going to exhibit this map in a textbook or classroom, what would you show along with it to help students understand its value? Why?

Post-Seminar Process

- Have participants write a self-assessment of their personal participation goal.
- Do a group assessment of the social and intellectual goals of seminar.
- Note reminders for next seminar.

Post-Seminar Content

- **Transition to writing:** Have participants take notes to brainstorm ideas that they heard, said, and thought during seminar related to the ideas under discussion (and the prewrite).
- **Writing task:** After examining and discussing a recent geological map of the state of Oklahoma, write an essay for the Oklahoma State Tourism Board in which you describe the geology of Oklahoma in at least three regions. Support your discussion with evidence from the text. (informational or explanatory/description, LDC Task #1E2)
- **Brainstorm:** Invite participants to talk in pairs for two minutes to share thoughts about what the writing task is asking and how they might respond.
- **Structuring the writing:** Allot a few minutes for all to sketch an outline for their writing. Draft the outline and use it to refine their thinking. Provide students with an outline template or templates as necessary to scaffold this stage.
- **First draft:** Challenge all to draft their descriptive essays by listing key points about the state's geologic regions. Refer to the original map in detail in order to illustrate key points.
- **Collaborative revision:** Have participants work in pairs to read their first drafts aloud to each other, with emphasis on reader as creator and editor. The listeners say back one point they heard clearly and ask one question for clarification. Have students switch roles. Give time for full revisions, resulting in a second draft.

- **Edit:** Once the second draft is complete, have participants work in groups of three or four, this time taking turns reading each other's second drafts slowly and silently, marking any spelling or grammar errors they find. (Have dictionaries and grammar handbooks available for reference.) Take this opportunity to clarify or reteach any specific grammar strategies you have identified as a need. Give time for full revisions, resulting in a third and final draft.
- **Publish:** Publish (either virtually or on paper) the final copies of the resulting personal essays in a collection to be shared with the Oklahoma State Tourism Board and used as exemplary personal essays for future students.

Note: For the specific version of the Geological Map of Oklahoma referenced in this plan, see www.ou.edu/ogs.

FROM *OPTICS* (BOOK III, PART 1) BY ISAAC NEWTON

Grade/subject: High school/science
Ideas, values: Deduction, experimentation, induction, science

Pre-Seminar Content

- **Launch activity:** Display definitions for *inductive* versus *deductive* thinking and have students write and explain several examples of both in their science journals.
- **Inspectional read:** Distribute the text and ask participants to anticipate what they expect this reading to be like. Read text aloud for the first time, while students note any unfamiliar vocabulary. Have participants number the eight sentences in the text.
- **Background:** Set the historical context by noting that Isaac Newton (1642–1727) was one of the most creative and influential mathematicians and scientists who ever lived (equivalent to Einstein in the extent to which he shaped our understanding of the world). He experimented on light from an early age and used geometric

principles to explore and explain its nature. His major work *Optics* appeared in a series of papers presented to the Royal Society between 1672 and 1676, which were collected and published in 1704. They contain what was one of the earliest (and therefore most radically controversial) statements of the scientific method.

- **Vocabulary development:** List the unfamiliar words or phrases (identified in the inspectional read) on the (interactive) whiteboard; be sure to include *natural philosophy, method of composition, hypotheses, compounds, ingredients,* and *synthesis.* Explain that students will need to understand the meaning of these terms during the seminar discussion and in order to complete the writing assignment (where they will use many of them in their own sentences). Divide the class into teams to define the words and share the definitions with the whole group while all take notes as necessary for understanding.

- **Analytical read:** Assign the eight sentences to the participants (in small groups) to paraphrase. Ask them to read the whole text a second time and then use the attached graphic organizer to paraphrase the sentence assigned to them. When they have finished their individual paraphrases, as a class go through the whole text, letting each group read their sentence and share their paraphrase. (Note that this is an inductive and analytical process—working from part to whole.)

Pre-Seminar Process

- Define and state purpose for Paideia seminar.
- Describe the responsibilities of facilitator and participants.
- Have participants set a personal goal.
- Agree on a group goal.

Seminar Discussion

Opening (identify main ideas from the text):

- What sentence or part of a sentence is most puzzling to you? (round-robin response)
- What is it you don't understand about that statement? (spontaneous discussion)

Core (analyze textual details):

- What is Newton saying about "method of analysis" as compared to "method of composition" in the first sentence?
- When Newton writes, in sentence 4, that the process of analysis is "the best way of arguing that the nature of things admits of," what does he mean? Do you agree?
- What does Newton say about "the argument" in sentence 7?
- If you were Newton's publisher and you wanted to promote his work, what title would you give to this important excerpt? Why?
- Newton wrote in an era when it was generally assumed that "truth" was handed down from those in authority (the church, the scholars, the royalty, etc.). How does this statement challenge that traditional way of looking at the world?

Closing (personalize and apply the textual ideas):

- What part of nature (large or small) would you like to better understand? How could you apply Newton's "method of analysis" to this subject?

Post-Seminar Process

- Have participants write a self-assessment of their personal participation goal.
- Do a group assessment of the social and intellectual goals of seminar.
- Note reminders for next seminar.

Post-Seminar Content

- **Transition to writing:** Have participants take notes to brainstorm ideas that they heard, read, and thought during seminar related to the ideas of induction versus deduction.
- **Writing task:** Why is inductive reasoning fundamental to science as a discipline? After reading and discussing an excerpt from Newton's *Optics* on inductive reasoning, write an article for an online science magazine in which you relate why Newton's "method of analysis, ought ever to precede the method of composition." Support your discussion with evidence from the text. (informational or explanatory/procedural-sequential, LDC Task #1E7)
- **Brainstorm:** Display the writing task and then have students talk in pairs for two minutes to share thoughts about what the writing task is asking and how they might respond. Discuss for clarity with the entire class.
- **Structuring the writing:** Ask students to design an outline for this multiparagraph essay based on the task. Encourage them to consider how best to explain Newton's arguments to a modern audience consisting mostly of high school students like themselves.
- **First draft:** Challenge all to draft their process analysis by writing the paragraphs defined by their outlines. Have them refer to the Newton text in detail for examples.
- **Collaborative revision:** Have participants work in pairs to read their first drafts aloud to each other, with emphasis on reader as creator and editor. (Stress that each paper must state a clear argument and support that position with evidence from the texts.) Listeners say back one point they heard clearly and ask one question for clarification. Have students switch roles. Give time for full revisions, resulting in a second draft.
- **Edit:** Once the second draft is complete, have participants work in groups of three or four, this time taking turns reading each other's second drafts slowly and silently, marking any spelling or grammar errors they find. (Have dictionaries and grammar

handbooks available for reference.) Take this opportunity to clarify or reteach any specific grammar strategies you have identified your students needing. Give time for full revisions, resulting in a third and final draft.

- **Publish:** Publish the final student essays in an online science magazine hosted on the class web site. Invite responses from other high school students around the world.

Note: This excerpt is drawn from *Optics* (Book III, Part 1) by Isaac Newton (1704).

"BODY RITUAL AMONG THE NACIREMA" BY HORACE MINER

Grade/subject: High school/social studies
Ideas, values: Custom, language, rhetoric, satire

Pre-Seminar Content

- **Launch activity:** Ask students if they brushed their teeth this morning. And then (assuming so) have them reflect on the details. What's the name of the toothpaste, how do they put the paste on the brush, and what are their brushing techniques? Then ask them to think about how they might describe what they did in a way that makes fun of how they performed this body ritual. Invite them to practice describing brushing their teeth (or another body ritual of their choice) to someone else with the intention of poking fun in a lighthearted way. After they practice, give them a few minutes to write a draft of their description. Review the definition of satire.
- **Inspectional read:** Distribute the text and have students take a look at the title. Ask them what they imagine the words to mean. Have students note the source and anticipate what this reading will be like. Have them number the paragraphs 1–10. Read the text aloud together.

- **Background:** Share that Horace Miner was an anthropologist. He wrote this article satirizing American culture and, as the *Encyclopedia of Social and Cultural Anthropology* states, "offered critiques of Euro-American arrogance, by showing that magic is not the prerogative of non-Western societies," as well as providing "a classic and apt example of how ethnocentrism can color one's thinking." Briefly note that anthropology is the study of human nature, and ethnocentrism is judging another culture solely by the values and standards of one's own culture.
- **Vocabulary development:** Briefly discuss ritual—doing something with deliberate meaning. Ask students what other words are unfamiliar and discuss. Have students write out *Nacirema* backward (near the title) and *latipso* (next to paragraph 6).
- **Analytical read:** Have students read the text a second time on their own and make note (in margins) of at least three modern-day words or terms that are implied in the reading; for example, next to paragraph 4, one might write *bathroom* as the modern term for *shrine*.

Pre-Seminar Process

- Define and state purpose for Paideia seminar.
- Describe the responsibilities of facilitator and participants.
- Have participants set a personal goal.
- Agree on a group goal.

Seminar Discussion

Opening (identify main ideas from the text):

- What phrase or sentence is most amusing to you? (round-robin response)
- What is it about that phrase that you find amusing? (spontaneous dialogue)

Core (analyze textual details):

- The last sentence in paragraph 2 reads: "its ceremonial aspects and associated philosophy are unique." What do you think that phrase suggests?
- What is your impression of the Nacirema culture based on paragraph 2 and the first sentence of paragraph 3?
- According to paragraphs 3 and 4, who is powerful?
- What does paragraph 6 say about this culture's belief about life and death?
- What does this article illustrate about the features of satirical writing?

Closing (personalize and apply the textual ideas):

- What is something that happens in our school day that we could describe satirically? How would you describe it?

Post-Seminar Process

- Have participants write a self-assessment of their personal participation goal.
- Do a group assessment of the social and intellectual goals of seminar.
- Note reminders for next seminar.

Post-Seminar Content

- **Transition to writing:** Have students take a few minutes and make note of important points that they thought, read, and heard during seminar.
- **Writing task:** After reading "Body Ritual Among the Nacirema," write a short essay in which you describe satire. Support your discussion with evidence from this article, *The Adventures of Huckleberry Finn,* or a real-life example. Imagine

your readers are young anthropologists. (informational or explanatory/description, LDC Task #1E2)

- **Brainstorm:** Have students talk in pairs about what the task is asking of them. Encourage note taking.
- **Structuring the writing:** Guide students in creating an outline or structure for their essay. Challenge them to think of what key points they will make and in what sequence. Remind students to refer to their notes.
- **First draft:** Challenge all to draft their process analysis by writing the paragraphs defined by their outlines. Refer to the Miner text in detail for examples.
- **Collaborative revision:** Have students work in pairs taking turns reading their essays. One person reads his or her essay aloud, and the partner listens. The readers should stop and make revisions as they come upon sections they want to change. Afterward, the listeners should say back one key point they heard. Have students switch roles.
- **Edit:** Once the second draft is complete, have participants work in groups of three or four, this time taking turns reading each other's second drafts slowly and silently, marking any spelling or grammar errors they find. (Have dictionaries and grammar handbooks available for reference.) Take this opportunity to clarify or reteach any specific grammar strategies you have identified your students needing. Give time for full revisions, resulting in a third and final draft (see student exemplar in Figure 10.3).
- **Publish:** Publish (either virtually or on paper) the final copies of the resulting essays in a collection of exemplary definition essays to be shared with future students. Circulate copies through both the class library and school media center.

Note: "Body Ritual Among the Nacirema" by Horace Miner (1956), *American Anthropologist*, 58(3), 503–507.

Figure 10.3

"Body Ritual Among the Nacirema" Student Exemplar

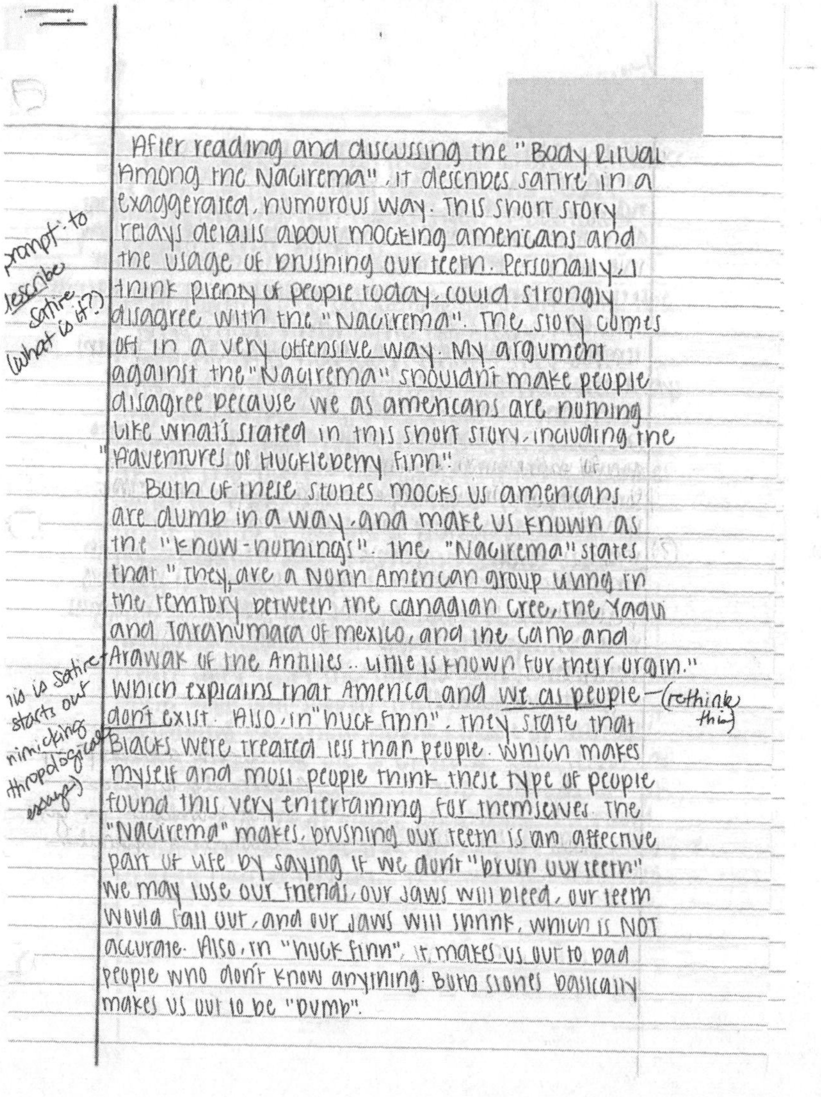

prompt: to describe satire (What is it?)

After reading and discussing the "Body Ritual Among the Nacirema", it describes satire in a exaggerated, humorous way. This short story relays details about mocking americans and the usage of brushing our teeth. Personally, I think plenty of people today, could strongly disagree with the "Nacirema". The story comes off in a very offensive way. My argument against the "Nacirema" shouldn't make people disagree because we as americans are nothing like what's stated in this short story, including the "Adventures of Huckleberry Finn".

Both of these stories mocks us americans, are dumb in a way, and make us known as the "know-nothings". The "Nacirema" states that "They are a North American group living in the territory between the canadian cree, the Yaqui and Tarahumara of mexico, and the carib and Arawak of the Antiles. Little is known for their origin." Which explains that America and we al people don't exist. Also in "huck finn", they state that Blacks were treated less than people. Which makes myself and most people think these type of people found this very entertaining for themselves. The "Nacirema" makes, brushing our teeth is an affective part of life by saying if we don't "brush our teeth" we may lose our friends, our jaws will bleed, our teeth would fall out, and our jaws will shrink, which is NOT accurate. Also, in "huck finn", it makes us out to bad people who don't know anything. Both stories basically makes us out to be "Dumb".

This is Satire starts out mimicking [an]thropological essay)

(rethink this)

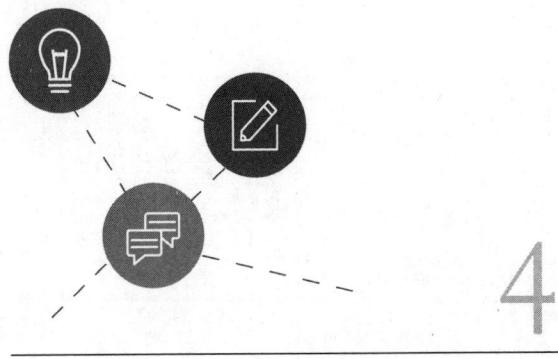

4

Appendixes

Appendix A

Glossary of Discourse and Writing Terms

Assignment: A prompt, rubric, and instructional plan designed to create a context for teaching and learning.

Controlling idea: The line of thought that is introduced in a written claim or thesis and carried throughout the composition.

Discourse: The use of speaking and listening skills to engage in academic "talk," whether discussions, conversations, or dialogue around ideas, topics, questions, and issues that take their cue from texts.

DWC: The Discourse and Writing Cycle, the framework for teaching discourse and writing that involves three complementary instructional sequences: the Discourse Sequence, the Transition to Writing Sequence, and the Writing Sequence. The DWC engages all the primary literacy skills: reading, speaking, listening, and writing. These skills, taught in concert, deliberately develop critical-thinking skills.

Essay: A formal composition in which the writer discusses an issue using argument or explanation modes. Writers in the humanities use this term most often when writing about literature, the arts, science, and history.

Expository writing: Nonfiction writing distinguished by a controlling idea, logic structure, and textual evidence in which writers use a rhetorical mode to present their topics to readers.

Fluency: Mastery in the flow of language, typically thought of in speech but also in writing. It can also mean adeptness in interpreting the written and spoken words of others.

Paideia seminar: A specific seminar process involving collaborative intellectual discourse facilitated with open-ended questions about a text. Consistent seminar practice nurtures basic speaking and listening as well as reading skills—and serves as a powerful introduction to writing. Taken together, this complex of literacy skills teaches critical thinking.

Prompt: A statement in which teachers initiate writing for a purpose and audience and specify a product. The prompt is the essential ingredient of a writing task, whether it is taught or assessed.

Report: A formal composition in which the writer uses evidence to inform or explain a topic or to argue a point. The term is used most often in science, business, and technical fields.

Seminar questions: Questions asked of participants by the teacher/ facilitator. Effective seminar questions have three fundamental characteristics: They are thought-provoking, clear, and open-ended. The Paideia seminar involves three types of questions: opening, core, and closing.

Structure: The way a composition's line of thought is organized, usually consisting of an opening, development or body, and closing. Structures can vary based on the purpose and audience.

Text: Human artifact that represents a set of significant and interrelated ideas. Texts can include books, problems, and experiments, as well as photographs, maps, paintings, and other works of art. The current emphasis on reading skills places a premium on texts in the form of printed language, but as we use it here, *text* does not exclude other forms of expression. An appropriate text for formal discussion and extended writing has four characteristics: intellectual richness, complexity, relevance, and ambiguity.

Thinking: The ability to explain and manipulate a text. By text, we mean a set of interrelated ideas, often represented in a human artifact. Learning to think, then, is the process of explaining and manipulating increasingly complex texts successfully. By definition, increasingly complex texts contain larger numbers of discrete elements and more complex relationships between those elements.

✦ ✦ ✦ ✦ ✦

Appendix B
The DWC Lesson Plan Template

(Note that in this template and the sample plans included in Chapter 10, the pre-seminar content reading strategies are included as well as the Discourse, Transition to Writing, and Writing Sequences. Close reading is a natural part of the Paideia seminar and precedes the DWC.)

Text:

Grade/subject:

Ideas, values:

PRE-SEMINAR CONTENT

- Launch activity:
- Inspectional read:
- Background:
- Vocabulary development:
- Analytical read:

PRE-SEMINAR PROCESS

- Define and state purpose for Paideia seminar.
- Describe the responsibilities of facilitator and participants.
- Have participants set a personal goal.
- Agree on a group goal.

SEMINAR DISCUSSION

Opening (identify main ideas from the text):

Core (analyze textual details):

Closing (personalize and apply the textual ideas):

POST-SEMINAR PROCESS

- Have participants write a self-assessment of their personal participation goal.
- Do a group assessment of the social and intellectual goals of seminar.
- Note reminders for next seminar.

POST-SEMINAR CONTENT

- Transition to writing:
- Writing task: (LDC Task #)
- Brainstorm:
- Structuring the writing:
- First draft:
- Collaborative revision:
- Edit:
- Publish:

Appendix C
Check Your Thinking

CHAPTER 2

Consider the following two prompts and compare their clarity and purpose. Try writing the opening paragraph for each prompt. Are the prompts clear and doable?

A. After reading *Johnny Tremain,* write an essay in which you compare the Lyte family to the Lorne family and explain how they help the reader understand a historical context. Support your discussion with evidence from the text.

B. Why do we need society? Discuss how the characters and the theme are related in *Lord of the Flies*.

Our Response

The first prompt provides students with a focused context for writing. It states a text and a product and provides a clear purpose (delineate, explain, and support). It is also aligned closely to Common Core RL.5.3 and W.2. The second prompt starts with a broad question that does not clearly relate to the text, providing too much room for students to write from opinion rather than from the text. We might argue that it's a biased question. As written, the prompt does not state a product and does not give enough specifics about what characters. It is only loosely aligned to RL.2. Ultimately, it doesn't give the student writer enough guidance.

CHAPTER 3

How do you see seminars fitting into a unit of study in your classroom?

Our Response

Seminars are designed to teach the ideas and values in your curriculum as well as the literacy skills required to think successfully about those ideas and values. Your first step should always be to identify the concepts that form the foundation of your subject in general and your unit curriculum in particular. From there, you should identify texts that embody those ideas and use them as the basis for close reading and seminar discussion. In this way, you will give your students texts that are rich in ideas—which in turn will reward the extended effort required to read closely and discuss deeply.

CHAPTER 4

What makes the outlining stage so important? How might you leverage this practice to teach thinking?

Our Response

To help students understand the practice of outlining as a thinking activity, have them outline texts and discuss any patterns of thought or structures they see. Discuss why these structures help the reader. Use this insight to help them develop their own outlines.

Mr. B., a 4th grade teacher who was having his students write in response to a math text, helped his students outline their response by providing them with a template. The template scaffolded the response using a series of generic sentence starters for the topic and supporting sentences. The students' work involved providing specific details relevant to the problem prompt. In this way, Mr. B. was able to teach paragraph structure while simultaneously helping students organize their thoughts. Over time, he applied a gradual release strategy to pull away the use of the template.

CHAPTER 5

Ms. Chavez, a high school teacher, sees 185 students a day in her history classes. Despite having so many students and therefore so many papers to read, she is determined to engage students in discourse and writing assignments. What might you suggest to Ms. Chavez to make her work manageable?

Our Response

Here is a short list of ways to face this common challenge:

- Give an assignment to half the class or half of your class periods during one week, and then assign the other half the next week.
- Assign students in small groups to a writing step. For example, as a group they might develop an outline; one student writes the initial draft, another works on the revisions, and another works on editing. They check back with each other after each step to discuss changes. Rotate students with each assignment.
- Limit what you score or give feedback on, for example, outlining and revision drafts.
- Use peer scoring and feedback sessions often, and provide specific instructions for these sessions.

CHAPTER 6

How does Maynard's full use of the Discourse and Writing Cycle encourage students to think about the science curriculum at a deeper level?

Our Response

Maynard uses the DWC to teach rigorous literacy skills and science content simultaneously, the epitome of disciplinary literacy. By teaching close reading, formal discussion, and extended writing in his science class, he is teaching both the ideas of science and the vocabulary with which to think and write about those ideas. In essence, he's teaching disciplinary thinking, in this case about scientific discovery and revolution.

CHAPTER 7

What values would you identify for a seminar in your class? What text might you choose to engage students in thinking about those values? What writing prompt would you then assign?

Our Response

If you chose "courage," for example, you might consider the following texts:

Tillie Olsen, "I Stand Here Ironing" (Middle School, High School)

William Butler Yeats, "Easter 1916" (Middle School, High School)

Homer, *The Iliad*, Book 1 (High School)

Emma Lazarus, "The New Colossus" (Elementary School, Middle School)

Prompt: Write an essay in which you examine the theme of courage in Olsen's essay "I Stand Here Ironing." Be sure to cite evidence from the text.

CHAPTER 8

What are the "big ideas" that you build your units of study around? When and how do you use discussion and writing as a means for your students to practice historical thinking about those ideas?

Our Response

You may choose to plan a unit around the following ideas: *citizen, equality,* and *justice*—situated within the American civil rights era. Your focus text might be Martin Luther King Jr.'s "Letter from a Birmingham Jail," leading to this writing task: Is Martin Luther King correct that the goal of America is freedom? After reading King's "Letter from a Birmingham Jail," write a letter to your congressperson in which you address the question and argue whether King is correct about the goal of America. Support your discussion with evidence from the text.

CHAPTER 9

Often assignments in these fields are interdisciplinary. What would it involve in your school if two teachers taught an assignment together? Review the following sample interdisciplinary assignment prompts and think about what roles each discipline might play.

Our Response

- *Science and math: Conduct an experiment in which you determine the chemical reaction when you combine any set of the three selected liquids. Write a lab report and include an explanation for each reaction.*

The science teacher conducts a seminar on chemistry followed by the experiment. The math teacher teaches the math involved in the experiment. They both teach aspects of the lab report that are relevant to their field.

- *Engineering and language arts: After participating in the seminar on bridges, conduct an experiment to determine the highest level of stress a bridge made of cardboard paper can withstand. Write a report detailing your experiment and your conclusion.*

The language arts teacher conducts a seminar on a series of famous bridge illustrations and the writing cycle. The engineering teacher teaches the experiment.

- *Mechanics and technology: Your lawn mower is costing you too much money to run. Write a short memo in which you determine which fuel is more efficient and document your process and findings.*

The mechanics and technology teachers plan together how to sequence the steps necessary for students to arrive at an informed

decision. They decide that the mechanics teacher will conduct the seminar on a diagram of a lawn mower and the technology teacher will use this as an opportunity to teach word processing skills to write the memo.

References

Adler, M. J. (1952). *The great ideas: Syntopicon*. Vols. 2–3. *Great books of the Western world*. Chicago: Encyclopedia Britannica.

Adler, M. J. (1982). *The Paideia proposal*. New York: Macmillan.

Adler, M. J. (1983). *How to speak, how to listen*. New York: Macmillan.

Adler, M. J. (1988). A declaration of principles by the Paideia Associates. In G. van Doren (Ed.), *Reforming education: The opening of the American mind* (pp. 309–310). New York: Macmillan.

Adler, M. J., & van Doren, C. (1972). *How to read a book: The classic guide to intelligent reading*. New York: Simon and Schuster.

Applebee, A. N., & Langer, J. A. (2013). *Writing instruction that works: Proven methods for middle and high school classrooms*. New York: Teachers College Press; Berkeley, CA: National Writing Project.

Bacon, F. (1601/1905). Of studies. In *The philosophical works of Francis Bacon*. (pp. 797–798). London: George Routledge and Sons.

Billings, L., & Roberts, T. (2012–2013). Think like a seminar. *Educational Leadership, 70*(4), 32–37.

Burke, J. (2003). *Writing reminders: Tools, tips, and techniques*. Portsmouth, NH: Heinemann.

Dougherty, E. (2012). *Assignments matter: Making the connections that help students meet standards*. Alexandria, VA: ASCD.

Emig, J. (1977). Writing as a mode of learning. *College Composition and Communication, 28*(2), 122–128.

Feldman, C. A., & Pittock, J. (n.d.). A closer look at "Mother to Son." Retrieved from https://coretools.ldc.org/mods/a6c48a89-72c3-4768-98b6-e7bdaecbba98

Fisher, D., Frey, N., & Rothenberg, C. (2008). *Content-area conversations: How to plan discussion-based lessons for diverse language learners*. Alexandria, VA: ASCD.

Harmon, W. (2012). *A handbook to literature* (12th ed.). New York: Longman.

He, J., Satyam, R., & Stehr, E. (2013). What do we mean by length, area, capacity, and volume? Retrieved from http://www.msu.edu/~stemproj/presentations/STEM_MiCTM_2013_JH_RS_ES_Dfns.pdf

Hutchins, R. M. (1952). *The great conversation: The substance of a liberal education*. Vol. 1. *Great books of the Western world*. Chicago: Encyclopedia Britannica, Inc.

Lanham, R. A. (2006). *Revising prose* (5th ed.). New York: Pearson-Longman Press.

Matsumura, L. C. (2005). *Creating high-quality classroom assignments*. Lanham, MD: ScarecrowEducation.

McDonald, C. R., & McDonald, R. L. (Eds.). (2002). *Teaching writing: Landmarks and horizons*. Carbondale, IL: Southern Illinois University Press.

McTighe, J., & Wiggins, G. (2013). *Essential questions: Opening doors to student understanding*. Alexandria, VA: ASCD.

Montaigne, M. E. de (1580/1952). *The essays of Michel Eyquem de Montaigne*. Vol. 25. *Great books of the Western world*. (Charles Cotton, Trans.). Chicago: Encyclopedia Britannica, Inc.

National Governors Association Center for Best Practices & Council of Chief State School Officers. (2010a). *Common core state standards for English language arts and literacy in history/social studies, science, and technical subjects*. Washington, DC: Authors.

National Governors Association Center for Best Practices & Council of Chief State School Officers. (2010b). *Common core state standards for mathematics*. Washington, DC: Authors.

Olson, B. (2013). College writing and LDC. Retrieved February 24, 2013, from http://www.literacydesigncollaborative.org

Olson, C. B. (2003). *The reading/writing connection: Strategies for teaching and learning in the secondary classroom*. Boston: Allyn and Bacon.

Radcliffe, T. (1972). Talk-write composition: A theoretical model proposing the use of speech to improve writing. *Research in the Teaching of English, 6*(2), 187–199.

Roberts, T., & Billings, L. (2003). *The Paideia seminar: Active thinking through dialogue in the secondary grades* (2nd ed.). Asheville, NC: National Paideia Center.

Roberts, T., & Billings, L. (2008). Thinking is literacy, literacy thinking. *Educational Leadership, 65*(5), 32–36.

Roberts, T., & Billings, L. (2012). *Teaching critical thinking: Using seminars for 21st century literacy*. Larchmont, NY: Eye on Education.

Schmoker, M. (2011). *Focus: Elevating the essentials to radically improve student learning*. Alexandria, VA: ASCD.

Sharrat, L., & Fullan, M. (2012). *Putting FACES on the data: What great leaders do!* Thousand Oaks, CA: Corwin Press.

Tennessee Department of Education. (2009). *Tennessee academic vocabulary: A guide for Tennessee educators*. Retrieved from http://www.tn.gov/education/ci/doc/VOCABULARY.pdf

Trefil, J. (1996). *101 things you don't know about science and no one else does either*. Boston: Houghton Mifflin.

Williams, E. H. (n.d.). Writing in the sciences. Retrieved from https://www.hamilton.edu/writing/writing-resources/writing-in-the-sciences

Williams, J. M., & Colomb, G. G. (2010). *Style: Lessons in clarity and grace* (10th ed.). Boston: Longman.

Zinsser, W. (1988). *Writing to learn*. New York: HarperCollins.

Zoellner, R. (1969). Talk-write: A behavioral pedagogy for composition. *College English, 30*(4), 267–330.

Zull, J. E. (2002). *The art of changing the brain: Enriching the practice of teaching by exploring the biology of learning*. Sterling, VA: Stylus Publishing.

Index

The letter *f* following a page number denotes a figure.

analytical read, pre-seminar, 129, 132,
   137–138, 142, 146, 150
articulation participation goal, 43*f*
assessment
   formative, 13
   post-seminar, 48–50, 130, 134, 139,
      142, 143, 147, 151
assignments. *See also* writing assignments
   defined, 157*d*
   sequences comprising, 37
assignments, to write effective
   content, identify, 21–22
   example, 31–32
   learning goals, identify, 22
   overview, 36*f*
   product, identify the, 24
   prompt challenges, add, 61
   prompts, write and test, 25–31
   revision, 34
   rhetorical mode, determine, 23–24
   rubrics, write and test, 30–31
   student work products, analyze, 33–34
   texts, identify, 22–23
attention participation goal, 43*f*

background, pre-seminar sharing, 127, 128,
   132, 142, 145, 149–150
blueprinting, 57
"Body Ritual Among the Nacirema" (Mil-
   ner) (language arts lesson plan), 149–153,
   153*f*
brainstorming, post-seminar, 130, 134, 139,
   144, 148, 151

career readiness, 8, 10, 94
celebration stage, 75–76
collaboration, post-seminar
   brainstorming, 130, 134, 139, 144,
      148, 151
   for draft revisions, 40, 72–75, 131, 134,
      140, 144, 148, 152
   editing stage, 131, 134, 140, 144, 148,
      152
college readiness, 8, 10, 94
Common Core State Standards (CCSS)
   classroom discussion in the, 123–124
   communication skills in the, 8
   English language arts on literacy, 14
   for Mathematical Practice, 123
   for narrative writing, 103
communication skills, need for, 8
complex texts, 8–11
computer tools, 74
connection participation goal, 44*f*
content, identify to write assignments, 21–22
controlling idea, 64–65, 157*d*
copyediting, 74
culture, discourse-writing, 12–14

democratic component of Paideia seminar,
   40
descriptive papers, writing, 122
disciplinary literacy, 9–10
discourse. *See also* discussion
   defined, 8, 157*d*
   writing relation to, 7, 10, 12–15

About the Authors

Eleanor Dougherty is a consultant with education foundations and agencies on curriculum and professional development. Her graduate degree is in literacy education with an emphasis on the teaching of writing. She has assisted districts and organizations with diverse student populations across the country, and her work over the last two decades has focused on literacy and its role in the larger curriculum, particularly in the core subjects. Dougherty is the author of books and articles on education, including the ASCD book *Assignments Matter: Making the Connections That Help Students Meet Standards*. She is currently involved in developing a national literacy strategy through the Literacy Design Collaborative. Eleanor can be reached at edthink.ecd@gmail.com.

Terry Roberts and **Laura Billings** are the director and associate director of the National Paideia Center (NPC), which provides transformative professional development across the United States and abroad. The NPC is widely celebrated as a primary source for materials and training on classroom dialogue at all levels and in all subjects. Roberts and Billings have written extensively about the relationship between seminar discussion and critical thinking, most recently in their book *Teaching Critical Thinking: Using Seminars for 21st Century Literacy*. They can be reached through the NPC website (www.paideia.org) or via e-mail at troberts@paideia.org and laura@paideia.org.

Related ASCD Resources

At the time of publication, the following ASCD resources were available (ASCD stock numbers appear in parentheses). For up-to-date information about ASCD resources, go to www.ascd.org. You can search the complete archives of *Educational Leadership* at http://www.ascd.org/el.

ASCD EDge®

Exchange ideas and connect with other educators interested in various topics, including literacy, on the social networking site ASCD EDge® at http://ascdedge.ascd.org/

Print Products

Assignments Matter: Making the Connections That Help Students Meet Standards by Eleanor Dougherty (#112048)

Teaching Writing in the Content Areas by Vicki Urquhart and Monette McIver (#105036)

Questioning for Classroom Discussion: Purposeful Speaking, Engaged Listening, Deep Thinking by Jackie Acree Walsh and Beth Dankert Sattes (#115012)

Student-Led Discussions: How do I promote rich conversations about books, videos, and other media? (ASCD Arias) by Sandi Novak (#SF114069)

Teaching Reading in the Content Areas: If Not Me, Then Who? by Vicki Urquhart & Dana Frazee (#112024)

For more information: send e-mail to member@ascd.org; call 1-800-933-2723 or 703-578-9600, press 2; send a fax to 703-575-5400; or write to Information Services, ASCD, 1703 N. Beauregard St., Alexandria, VA 22311-1714 USA.

ASCD's Whole Child approach is an effort to change the conversation about education from a focus on narrowly defined academic achievement to one that promotes the long term development and success of children. Through this approach, ASCD helps educators, families, community members, and policymakers move from a vision about educating the whole child to sustainable, collaborative action.

Whole Child Tenets

- Each student enters school **healthy** and learns about and practices a healthy lifestyle.
- Each student learns in an environment that is physically and emotionally **safe** for students and adults.
- Each student is actively **engaged** in learning and is connected to the school and broader community.
- Each student has access to personalized learning and is **supported** by qualified, caring adults.
- Each student is **challenged** academically and prepared for success in college or further study and for employment and participation in a global environment.

The Better Writing Breakthrough: Connecting Student Thinking and Discussion to Inspire Great Writing relates to the **engaged** and **challenged** tenets.

For more about the Whole Child approach, visit www.wholechildeducation.org.

DON'T MISS A SINGLE ISSUE OF ASCD'S AWARD-WINNING MAGAZINE,

EL EDUCATIONAL LEADERSHIP

If you belong to a Professional Learning Community, you may be looking for a way to get your fellow educators' minds around a complex topic. Why not delve into a relevant theme issue of *Educational Leadership*, the journal written by educators for educators.

Subscribe now, or buy back issues of ASCD's flagship publication at **www.ascd.org/ELbackissues.**

Single issues cost $7 (for issues dated September 2006–May 2013) or $8.95 (for issues dated September 2013 and later). Buy 10 or more of the same issue, and you'll save 10 percent. Buy 50 or more of the same issue, and you'll save 15 percent. For discounts on purchases of 200 or more copies, contact **programteam@ascd.org**; 1-800-933-2723, ext. 5773.

To see more details about these and other popular issues of *Educational Leadership*, visit **www.ascd.org/ELarchive.**

LEARN. TEACH. LEAD.

1703 North Beauregard Street
Alexandria, VA 22311-1714 USA

www.ascd.org/el